Marshall Trimble's Official

ARIZONA

TRIVIA™

Marshall Trimble

GOLDEN WEST
WEST ☼
PUBLISHERS

Front cover photos:

(Top row left) Lincoln Ragsdale; *(Top row center / left)* Ben Johnson; *(Top row center / right)* John Wayne; *(Top row right)* Rose Mofford.

(Bottom row left) Rex Allen, Sr.; *(Bottom row center)* Frank Luke; *(Bottom row right)* Danny White.

Dedication

To my good friend and colleague, Doug Clark, who followed his dream and with tireless effort and dogged determination brought the Arizona Trivia® Board Game to fruition and great success and, as a result, this book.

*Cactus art on pages 57, 58 & 61 from **Cactus Country**, by Jim Willoughby, also published by Golden West Publishers.*

Unless otherwise indicated, all photos were provided by the Maricopa Community College Southwest Studies Program

Library of Congress Cataloging-in-Publication Data

Trimble, Marshall
    Marshall Trimble's Official Arizona Trivia.
        p.   cm.
    Includes glossary & Index
        1. Arizona—Miscellanea.   2. Arizona—History—Miscellanea
I. Title.
F811.T765 1996   96-1766
979.1—dc20   CIP

Printed in the United States of America

ISBN #1-885590-05-9

Information in this book is deemed to be authentic and accurate by authors and publisher. However, they disclaim any liability incurred in connection with the use of information appearing in this book.

Golden West Publishers, Inc.
4113 N. Longview Ave.
Phoenix, AZ 85014, USA
(602) 265-4392

ARIZONA TRIVIA

Table of Contents

Introduction

What is Trivia?

Webster's defines trivia as "matters or things that are very unimportant, inconsequential, or non-essential." Actually, trivia goes far beyond those narrow boundaries. Trivia can, when used properly, be a wonderful source of interesting information on subjects off the general mainstream. Besides, what is "unimportant, inconsequential or non-essential" to some might be just the opposite to others, especially those interested in esoteric subjects.

Trivia, to be good, should have a zinger in the answer that creates a response like, "Gee, I didn't know that!" "Say, that's interesting!" or something similar. One of the best examples of what I consider good trivia on a subject unrelated to Arizona came from one of my college students who asked one day, "Who was Ted Williams' wingman during the Korean War?" In order for trivia to really work the answer should have significance, and it does. Ted Williams' wingman was John Glenn. This is trivia at its best. Ted Williams was one of America's most famous baseball players during the early 1950's when he was returned to action as a Marine fighter pilot. At the time young John Glenn was an unknown rookie pilot, destined to become the first American astronaut to fly into outer space.

Not all trivia questions are going to be that good—that one is a classic—but I always try to keep that concept in the back of my mind when creating trivia questions. It's my hope that you'll find these questions and answers both enlightening and fun.

Marshall Trimble

Arizona Trivia Sampler

1. In what city was the "Gunfight at OK Corral"?
2. What city took its name as the result of a card game?
3. In what city was the infamous Territorial Prison?
4. What famous copper mining city began an infamous "slide" down the mountain in the 1920's?
5. Fill in the missing lyric from this classic tune, *"Get Your Kicks On Route 66,"* "Flagstaff, Arizona, don't forget ....
6. Where was the first territorial capital of Arizona?
7. What city was known as the "Old Pueblo"?
8. What city owes its name to a firebird?
9. What city was known as the "Queen of the Copper Camps"?
10. Who was the first (and only) native Arizonan to be nominated by a major party for the Presidency of the United States?
11. Name the highest mountains in Arizona.
12. Which national forest will dull a logger's ax faster than any other?
13. What humorist took a look at a dry Arizona lake and mused, "If that was my lake, I'd mow it"?
14. What highway traversing the state was referred to by writer John Steinback as the "Mother Road"?
15. What city was originally called Flagpole?

(see answers page 6)

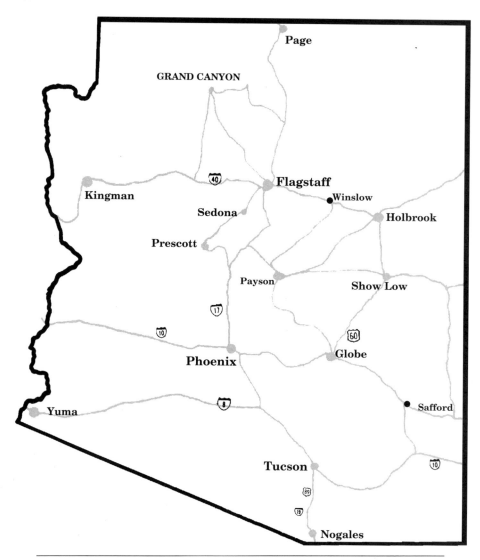

Answers to Sampler Questions (page 5)

1. Tombstone
2. Show Low
3. Yuma
4. Jerome
5. Winona
6. Prescott
7. Tucson
8. Phoenix
9. Bisbee
10. Barry Goldwater
11. The San Francisco Mountains (Mt. Humphrey's Peak is 12,633 feet.)
12. The Petrified Forest National Park.
13. Will Rogers
14. Route 66
15. Flagstaff

The Grand Canyon State

*Everything you wanted to know about Arizona
but were afraid to ask . . .*

The origin of the name *Arizona* has been traced to a small Tohono O'odham village or *rancheria,* about 25 miles southwest of today's Nogales. The original name, **Ali-Shonak,** described a small spring. At the time the Spanish called the region south of the Gila River, *Pimeria Alta,* or "Land of the Upper Pima." The mysterious land north of the Gila was generally referred to as *Tierra Incognita.* It was a forbidding place that was home to the Apache, Navajo, Quechan, Mojave and other native tribes.

The rugged mountains north of the village of Ali-Shonak was the site of a fabulous silver discovery in 1736. The name Ali-Shonak didn't roll easily off the Spanish tongue. They called it **Arissona.** Word spread quickly and Spanish miners or *gambusinos* poured into the area to seek their fortune. The rich native silver was described as "soft as wax." The strike became known as the *Planchas de Plata* (slabs or planks of silver.) One slab reportedly weighed more than a ton. The mining district became known as *Real de Arissona.*

Soon thousands of prospectors were trying their hand with lady luck in what could be called the West's first boom town. Spanish law decreed that the royal crown was to receive a *quinto (20%),* tax on any silver found and, in an effort to thwart the unlawful pilfering, authorities tried to slap on an embargo. But that didn't stop the prospectors, who cared little for bureaucrats or tax collectors. They managed to highgrade most of the silver by 1741 when, by royal order, the mines were closed. By that time, the mines had pretty much played out, but the name *Arissona* stuck.

When the Mexican War ended in 1848, the Treaty of Guadalupe Hidalgo gave the United States the land north of the Gila River. In 1850, it became a part of the Territory of New Mexico. Four years later, the Gadsden Purchase added the land south of the Gila to the present boundary. Before the ink was dry, Americans, "boomers and sooners," were prospecting for silver in the mountains south of Tucson. *Arissona* didn't roll off the Anglo tongues smoothly so they corrupted the name once again, to **Arizona.**

During the late 1850's, the western part of the New Mexico Territory began clamoring for a separate territory. W. Claude Jones, a roguish womanizer, politician and poet of sorts, is credited with naming the place Arizona. In 1856, when early settlers began petitioning for territorial status, Jones was the first to officially use the name.

Several names were suggested, including Gadsonia, (for the Gadsden Purchase). Fortunately, good sense prevailed and the folks settled on Arizona. The name became official with the creation of the **Territory of Arizona** in 1863.

During the 19th century, immigrants moved to Arizona from all directions. Miners and prospectors drifted in from California during the backwash of the Gold Rush. During the 1870's the Mormons began colonizing from Utah. Mexicans moved north, primarily seeking work in the mines and ranches. Texans and New Mexicans moved their cattle operations into the pristine rangelands during the latter part of the century.

Arizona is roughly the size of Italy. However, Arizona has a lot more breathing space. Italy has a population of about 55 million while Arizona has about 4 million. Arizona ranks 25th in population among the 50 states. **The Arizona Strip,** bounded on the north by the Utah border, the east by the Kaibab Plateau, the west by Nevada and the south by the Grand Canyon, is 14,000 sq. mi. in size but has a population of only 3,000—and they reside in a couple of communities. Apply the same ratio to New York City and it would have a population of only sixteen residents. *¡Carumba!* That would knock a hole in their crime problem. A resident of Moccasin, in Mohave County, on the Strip, would have to drive nearly 360 miles and cross three states just to get to the Mohave County seat at Kingman. As the crow flies, (if he flies over the Grand Canyon) it's only about 140 miles.

Dick Wick Hall, *"Sage of Salome,"* bragged that Salome was the only town in Arizona to experience an annual growth of 100%—19 people in 19 years.

Arizona's shape is almost square, the maximum north-south distance is 393 miles and the maximum east-west distance is 338 miles. The **total area** is 113,909 sq. miles, with about 492 square miles of surface water. The land slopes in a southwesterly direction towards Yuma. Over 90% of the land drains into the Colorado River.

The **highest point** in Arizona is Mt. Humphreys (12,633 ft) in the San Francisco Peaks near Flagstaff. The **lowest elevation** is around sea level near Yuma. The average elevation is 4,000 ft.

The **geographic center** is in Bloody Basin and the nearest large city to the center is beautiful downtown Bumble Bee. Newcomers and tenderfeet should not be taken in by that ubiquitous barroom bet that asks what's in the middle of Arizona. Take the bet; then tell 'em a "Z" is in the middle of AriZona.

Contrary to popular belief, *But It's A Dry Heat!* is *not* the state motto. The state **motto** is *Ditat Deus* or "God Enriches." The state **flower** is the saguaro blossom. The **colors** are blue and gold. The state **tree** is the paloverde and the state **bird** is the cactus wren. The state **gem** is turquoise; state **reptile** is the ridge-nosed rattlesnake; the state **fossil** is petrified wood and the state **mammal** is the ringtail cat.

The state **seal,** adopted in 1911, shows a sunrise (or sunset) over mountain peaks; a miner with a pick and shovel, representing mining (he's actually George Warren, who played a part in the discovery of the Copper Queen mine in Bisbee. He lost his share of the mine in a drunken wager when he bet he could outrun a horse in a race up Brewery Gulch); agriculture is represented by the irrigated field and grazing cattle; a dam with a reservoir behind it is a reminder that this is a desert and without the water, we'd all have to live elsewhere.

The **official neckwear** is the bola tie. Vic Cedarstaff, of Wickenburg, created the modern bola tie in 1949. He was also the first to market the tie around the world. Long-time television news anchor, Bill Close, was responsible for popularizing the bola.

The **official state song** is the *Arizona March Song*, but the alternate state song, *I Love You Arizona,* by Rex Allen Jr. is easier to sing and more popular.

The state even has an **official balladeer,** Dolan Ellis, long-time resident and original member of the New Christy Minstrels.

Arizona's nicknames include "the Valentine State." It became a state on **February 14, 1912,** and was the last of the contiguous territories to gain statehood. It has also been dubbed the "Copper State" as it produces most of the nation's copper. And the "Grand Canyon State," for its glorious gully. For many years it was called the "Baby State." That was before Alaska and Hawaii joined the Union in the 1950's. California still calls us the baby state. That's because we're always howlin' about all the water the gluttonous Californians pilfer from our river. In recent years, thanks to a few politicians, Arizona was known as the "State of Confusion."

The state **flag** is red, blue and gold with a copper star. The red and gold represent the colors carried by the first Spanish conquistadors.

The bottom half is blue, same as the national flag. The 13 red and gold rays are the same as the 13 stripes on the national flag. The top segment represents the rays of an Arizona sunset, and the copper star represents, historically, the state's most important industry. The flag was designed in 1910 by Captain Charles W. Harris. The first flag was sewn by Nancy Hayden, aka "Betsy Ross of Arizona." She was the wife of sheriff, and later U.S. Senator, Carl Hayden. On February 27, 1917, the state adopted it as the official flag of Arizona. There was some protest by some at the time who claimed it too closely resembled the rising sun flag of Japan.

Carl Hayden— (1910), when he was Sheriff of Maricopa County. Hayden served in the U. S. Congress for 57 continuous years— longer than any other politician in history.

(Photo courtesy Arizona Historical Foundation at ASU)

Bragging is a cherished right in Arizona

In land size, Arizona is the **6th largest state in the Union.** All of New England plus Pennsylvania and Delaware would fit inside its borders. There are at least 91 nations in the world smaller than Arizona. The entire state of Massachusetts would fit inside Maricopa County. The Navajo Reservation of northern Arizona is larger than Connecticut, New Hampshire and Massachusetts combined. Arizona has more parks and national monuments than any other state. She possesses the largest stand of ponderosa pine in the world, more mountains than Switzerland (not higher, just more) and more golf courses than Scotland.

Arizona is truly a land of anomalies (and tamales). Arizona has more sunshine than Florida and frequently has both the hottest and coldest temperatures on the same day. Mt. Lemmon, near Tucson, is the nation's southernmost ski resort. The state's **average rainfall** ranges from 3 inches in the desert near Yuma to 30 inches in the high country. We have dehydrated rivers; trees made of stone; cactus that blooms only at night; a bird that can run faster than it can fly; the only poisonous species of lizard in the nation; a river named Colorado that spends most of its time in Arizona; a retirement community named Youngtown; a Maricopa county and the town of Maricopa in Pinal County. Fort Apache is in Navajo County and the city of Navajo is in Apache County.

In 1944 a group of German prisoners of war plotted an escape from a compound situated not far from the Salt River. Three of them built a small boat and made plans to float down the Salt to the Gila, then on to the Colorado and Mexico. They tunneled out, and carrying their boat headed for the river. They were captured sitting there in that dry riverbed waiting for the tide to come in. To this day, those three men are known in Germany as the "Crazy Boatmen of Arizona."

The **population of Arizona** in 1995 was over 4 million people, most of whom seem to congregate in their motor vehicles every evening at 5 o'clock on the streets of downtown Phoenix. It's so crowded that if you want to hit a pedestrian, you have to get out of your car to do it. Will Rogers had the best solution, "Don't let people drive their cars until they're paid for."

Arizona, world-famous for its wide-open spaces is, in reality, an urban state. Some 80% live in towns or cities, the vast majority of those in Tucson or the greater-Phoenix area. Still, because of the vast size, there are only about 25 people per square mile in the state.

The state has **15 counties.** Coconino, the largest county at 18,540 sq. miles, is larger than New Hampshire, Delaware and Maryland combined. Maricopa County at 9,000 sq. miles is larger than Massachusetts.

The **world's deepest dam** (over 320 feet deep) is Parker Dam on the Colorado River.

At the **Four Corners,** the states of Utah, New Mexico, Colorado and Arizona come together. You can sprawl out on the monument and be in four states at the same time!

Tonto Natural Bridge, the **world's largest travertine bridge,** measures more than 500 feet. This limestone arch near Pine is a state park.

Less than 18% of the land in Arizona is privately owned. Nearly 27% is Indian land; 12.18% is state owned and 43.52% is federally owned.

The ethnic breakdown in the state is: Anglo, 80.8%; American Indian, 5.6%; Black, 3%; Asian, 1.5%; and other races, 9.1%. Those of Hispanic origin, 18.8%, can be of any race. According to the 1990 census, Arizona's population contained 29% minorities.

Wing Ong of Phoenix was the first Chinese-American in the U.S. elected to a state legislature (1966). That same year **Clovis Campbell** became the first African-American elected to the Arizona legislature. **Raul Castro,** born in Cananea, Sonora, was the first Hispanic elected governor of Arizona (1974). **Willie Wong,** elected in 1992, was the first Asian-American mayor of an Arizona city (Mesa) and **Coy Payne** of Chandler elected in 1990, the first African-American mayor.

Arizonans are a relatively young group. The state falls slightly below the national average **median age of 33.0.**

The **largest employer** in the state is the State of Arizona with over 22,000 employees. The second largest employer is Motorola, with 21,000 employees.

The **largest industry** is manufacturing and the leading job-producing industry is tourism.

Historically Arizona's strongest economic support came from the Four C's—**cotton, copper, cattle** and **citrus.** In recent years a fifth, **climate,** has been added.

Few areas of the world have a greater variety of wildlife. Arizona has 60% of all types of wildlife species found in North America. Ten species of **big game** found in the state include: javelina, bear, elk, antelope, big horn sheep, bison, mule deer, white tail deer, mountain lion and turkey.

Prescott claims the **oldest continuous *professional* rodeo** in America. Payson claims to have the **oldest *continuous* rodeo** in America.

The **religious affiliations** of Arizonans according to a 1991 study indicate that 23.9% are Catholic; 11.6% are Baptist; 6.6%, Methodist; 5.7%, Lutheran; 4.9%, Mormon; 2.9%, Presbyterian; 1.6%, Jewish; 1.4%, Episcopalian; 1.3%, Pentecostal. 12.2% claimed "no religion" and 27.9% are listed as "other."

The **oldest Protestant church** in Arizona (built in 1882) is St. Paul's Episcopal church in Tombstone.

The **oldest Catholic church** still in use is San Xavier del Bac, near Tucson. It was constructed between 1783 and 1797.

Speaking of churches, Holbrook gained the dubious distinction in the early days as Arizona's only county seat without a church. The town was founded in 1881 and went 32 years without a church. Finally, in 1913, at the urging of his wife, Sidney Sapp launched a drive to build one.

Although they have only been in Arizona since 1988, the **Arizona Cardinals** are the nation's **oldest continuous professional football franchise,** dating back to 1898.

Billy The Kid gunned down his first man, Frank "Windy" Cahill, at Fort Grant on August 17, 1877, after the latter called him a dirty name.

In 1899, along the Gila River, near today's Kearny, a diminutive young woman named **Pearl Hart** pulled the last stagecoach robbery (not counting the entertaining versions of Rawhide and Old Tucson) in America. She served time at the Yuma Territorial Prison then used her notoriety to launch an unsuccessful stage career.

On June 6, 1936, the first barrel of **tequila** produced in the United States rolled off the production line in Nogales.

Round Valley High School (Springerville-Eagar) has the nation's **first domed athletic facility** (for a high school). The J. Lawrence Walkup Sky Dome at Northern Arizona University in Flagstaff, where the Lumberjacks play their home football games, boasts the **world's largest wood-dome structure.**

The **last volcanic eruption** in Arizona occurred at Sunset Crater, near Flagstaff in A.D. 1064.

Oraibi, a Hopi Indian village on Third Mesa, dates back to before A.D. 1200 and is believed to be the **longest continuously inhabited community in the nation.**

The **Grand Canyon,** nature's grandest architectural masterpiece, is 227 miles long, one mile deep, with an average width of 10 miles. The Colorado River winds 277 miles through the canyon. The geological layers present a layer by layer record, a vertical mile of planetary history. Deep in the gorge are seen the worn down remains of mountains that towered majestically over this land two billion years ago.

The **best preserved meteor crater in America** is located near Winslow. Nearly 50,000 years ago a huge nickel-iron ball, weighing a few hundred thousand tons and traveling at a speed upwards of 5 to 10 miles per second slammed into the earth with such force that it destroyed all life for a hundred mile radius. The crater measures 4,150 feet rim-to-rim and is 570 feet deep.

Arizona has an interesting assortment of place names!

Phoenix was named for the mythical Egyptian bird that rose from the ashes of its own funeral pyre to be reborn. Modern Phoenix was built over the ruins of an advanced prehistoric civilization we call the Hohokam that flourished for centuries then mysteriously vanished.

Flagstaff takes its name from a flag-raising ceremony commemorating the nation's 100th anniversary of the signing of the Declaration of Independence. A party of colonists from Boston (how appropriate) was camped at the foot of the San Francisco Peaks on July 4, 1876.

Prescott was named for the historian, William Hickling Prescott, beating out Gimletville as the people's choice.

Tucson was the Spanish corruption of the Indian words *Chuk-Shon,* which described the "Dark Base At The Foot Of A Nearby Mountain."

Yuma is a corruption of the Quechan word, *Umo* or "smoke." It seems the early natives used smoky firebrands to ward off mosquitoes. Yuma, named for the Indian tribe living at the legendary river crossing, was a riverport town during the heyday of the steamboats on the Colorado River.

Sierra Vista used to be called Frye. Nobody wanted to admit to moving to "Frye" in Arizona so they changed it.

Some of Arizona's place names are picturesquely whimsical. **Show Low** reputedly got its name as a result of a card game. Two ranchers, Marion Clark and Corydon Cooley, felt the neighborhood was getting too crowded so they played a card game called Seven Up to see who would move. Low card won the hand. Clark said to Cooley, "If you show low, you win." Cooley drew the deuce of clubs and said, "Show low it is..." and Show Low it was.

Soldiers from Fort Apache named **Pinetop** for a tall, bushy-headed bartender.

The state has not one, but two mountain peaks named for General Edward O.C. Ord, who had a less than distinguished career in the territory during the Apache Wars. Among his limited number of supporters were some surveyors and map makers.

The town of **Why** sits out on the lonesome desert near Ajo. It was named by weary residents responding to tourists continually asking "Why would anybody want to live here?" **Lousy Gulch** got its name after all the residents contracted lice.

Charlie **McMillan** really tied one on that night in Globe. Legend has it he tried, unsuccessfully, to hit the ground with his hat, five times. The next day he and his partner, Dorey Harris, went out prospecting. They hadn't gone far when Charlie's hangover got the best of him and he lay down to sleep. While Charlie was in deep slumber, Dorey started picking at rocks nearby. By a stroke of prospector's luck, he managed to uncover a vast body of silver ore. A boom town materialized on the spot and they named it McMillan. The two million dollars taken out was owed to a bad hangover.

Soldiers from **Fort Huachuca** told prospector Ed Schieffelin that all he'd find out in that wild country around the San Pedro River was his tombstone. Victorio and his Apache warriors were on the prod at the time. Ed found silver instead and **Tombstone** became Arizona's greatest silver boom camp—and immortality as the, "Town Too Tough To Die."

Tombstone's notorious **Allen Street** was named, not for a gun-slinger, but for John "Pie" Allen. When the town hit pay dirt, the entrepreneurial Allen made his fortune selling homemade dried-apple pies to the hungry miners for a dollar apiece. Allen made the trivia list by being the first person to file for a homestead in the new Arizona Territory back in 1863.

That deep abyss between Flagstaff and Winslow, **Canyon Diablo,** was well-named. The devilish namesake located just east of the 220 foot-deep chasm was so bad old timers claimed you could walk a block in any direction and never leave the scene of a crime. By comparison, Holbrook and Tombstone look like a kid's summer camp. In just one year in Canyon Diablo (1881-1882) more men were killed in gun-fights, murders and robberies than Dodge City, Abilene and Tombstone combined.

Hell Street, the main (and only) street, stretched for a mile along the Santa Fe tracks, boasted 14 saloons, 10 gambling dens, four bordellos and two dance halls. Several years after the town gave up the ghost, 35 graves were found in the cemetery. All had died violently. All were men except for one woman, a prostitute named Clabberfoot Mary.

Total Wreck owes its name to an ugly outcropping of rocks that hung above the town. Some of Arizona's other physical features got their names from whimsical pioneers. Cowboys named **Wet Bottom Creek** because you couldn't drive cattle across it without getting wet up to your.....er bottom. I've never heard a cowboy refer to that part of one's anatomy as a "bottom." I'm sure you know what they really called it.

Another place name that couldn't be repeated in the presence of a lady was the **S.H. Mountains** in the Kofa range. Areas of the mountains resembled houses with little outhouses in back. Because of this unusual feature, the miners dubbed them with the obvious. When the women arrived the name was shortened to S.H. and that's how it's seen on most maps today.

Arizona has over a hundred thousand place names and these are just a sampling. Each one has a story to tell.

The foregoing may not cover "everything you've always wanted to know about Arizona but were afraid to ask", but it's a good start.

In Arizona, it's considered coarse manners to correct a liar

A well-known literary prodigy in the art of prevarication was Dick Wick Hall of Salome. He claimed his town's mascot was a seven-year-old frog that had never learned to swim, because, "he didn't need to." This community also boasted of a golf course called the Greasewood Lynx that was 247 miles long and had a par of 16,394. The clubhouse not only rented golf clubs, but camping equipment, maps, canteens and pack mules.

Arizona is covered with cactus, chaparral, sagebrush, canyons and a lot of hot air. Sherwin Williams claims credit for the Painted Desert; Frank Lloyd Wright for the design of the Grand Canyon; and Del Webb says they built it; Payson claims its climate is so healthy they had to shoot somebody just to start a cemetery; Gila Bend claims it sells more waterpumps and fanbelts for cars than anywhere else in the world; Bullhead City claims it's really Alpine, but nobody's buying it. Yuma has the best sense of *Yuma* and a Mexican food restaurant in Tucson claims the chile peppers in its servings are so hot you burn calories as you eat.

Arizona also has the driest rivers in the nation. The Agua Fria River has produced a rare species of native trout that *cannot swim*. Gila Bend is home to a species called *canteen fish*. They have a hump-reservoir on their back similar to camels. When their water hole dries up, they travel overland until they find another. The canteen keeps 'em from getting too thirsty on their journey. The only thing drier than the rivers is the *heat*!

Winslow holds the record for the longest continuous wind (it hasn't stopped yet); Ashfork, a town so small it has to share its horse with Seligman, claims the strongest wind. When it was founded in

1882, Ashfork was only 12 miles east of Kingman. Today it's 94 miles east. It's figured that sometime during the next century, Ashfork will be somewhere in New Mexico.

The **hottest recorded day in Phoenix** was June 26, 1990, when the temperature hit 122 degrees. How hot was that? The mayors of the outlying communities around Phoenix had a contest to see who had the hottest temperature. I had the pleasure of judging the claims of the outlying mayors. **Kent Wick** of Paradise Valley, won third place by claiming it was so hot his patio furniture was standing on one leg. Second place was won by the mayor of Scottsdale, **Herb Drinkwater,** who insisted he saw a jumping cactus in his yard leap into the swimming pool.

The winner was Tempe mayor, and native Arizonan, **Harry Mitchell.** He swore he saw a saguaro cactus pull itself up by the roots, walk over and hunker down in the shade of a mesquite tree. The winner was given an all-expense paid week in July at Gila Bend. Second place got two weeks in Gila Bend. Third place, predictably, got three weeks. *Remember, though, it's a dry heat.*

Nellie Cashman—prospector and restaurateur, was known affectionately throughout the West as the "angel of the mining camps". A pretty woman, she never married. Nellie preferred the free life of a prospector and adventurer. Her travels took her from Mexico to the Arctic Circle.

(Photo courtesy Arizona Historical Society / Tucson)

Commodore Perry Owens—Sheriff, Apache County (1887) — brought in by county officials during the Pleasant Valley war, he was considered by most to be a celebrated, legendary hero. There were those, too, who considered him a hired assassin.

(Photo courtesy Arizona State Library)

General Trivia Questions

1) What is Arizona's best-known nickname?
2) Name Arizona's five C's.
3) What is the largest Indian tribe in the United States?
4) Which city is higher in elevation, Tucson or Phoenix?
5) Where does one find trees that have turned to stone?
6) What Indian tribe calls itself a nation?
7) What are the well-known colorful Hopi Indian dolls called?
8) What is the water project bringing water to central Arizona from the Colorado River?
9) What popular liquor comes from the desert plant maguey (m'gay)?
10) What Arizona-based magazine has approximately 85% of its circulation outside of Arizona?
11) What is Arizona's "official neckware" (for men)?
12) What is Arizona's rainy season called?
13) What is iron pyrite commonly called?
14) Where were the men who "died with their boots on" frequently buried?
15) What Indian tribe lives at Fort McDowell?
16) Name Arizona's largest employer.
17) What is the oldest building on the University of Arizona campus?
18) Arizona's "Agua Fria Freddie Day" is synonymous with what national day?
19) Which architect is known for his wind bells?
20) The wood from which desert tree is in vogue for grilling steaks?
21) What is the English translation of Santa Cruz (County)?
22) What is Arizona's number one farm crop?
23) Name the University that has both an East and West campus.
24) What is the newest State Park in Arizona?
25) What is the Spanish word for fort?

26) What Phoenix museum is world renowned for its collection of Indian culture?

27) Members of what Indian tribe live at the bottom of the Grand Canyon?

28) Name the largest capital city in the U.S.

29) Name the first black person elected to the Arizona Senate.

30) To call a person a "Hassayamper" is a polite way of saying that one is a _____ ?

31) What facility found in most hospitals does Sun City's Boswell Memorial Hospital lack?

32) What brick is made from mud and straw?

33) What is Arizona's motto?

34) Who is the keeper of the "Great Seal of Arizona?"

35) Why is the Hopi Snake Dance performed?

36) What Indian tribe lives on the San Carlos Indian Reservation?

37) What city claims to be the home of the world's oldest continuous professional rodeo?

38) On what date did Arizona become a state? (Month, day and year)

39) What art or craft did the Navajo people learn from the Spaniards?

40) Name the first community college in America owned and operated by an Indian tribe.

41) Phoenix artist Jeanne Boylan made a famous sketch of the suspect in the FBI's largest manhunt ever. Who was that suspect known as?

42) What is an underground Hopi Indian ceremonial room called?

43) What is the stone bowl used by Indians to grind corn called?

44) What Arizona university is owned by the Arizona Southern Baptist Convention?

45) How did Tucson's Speedway Boulevard get its name?

46) What Arizona dam is formed by three concrete half-domes that resemble submerged eggs?

47) How many colors are in the state flag?

48) What is the name of the weather vane atop the State Capitol?

49) What metal covers the dome of Arizona's State Capitol?

50) What is the Spanish name for a lighted candle in a paper bag (popular at Christmas)?

51) What is the governing body of Arizona's three state universities?

52) What is the common name used to describe Arizona's long-stemmed cotton?

53) What interstate highway connects Phoenix with Flagstaff?

54) What is the science of tree ring dating which was made famous at the University of Arizona?

55) What is the name of the Mexican fry bread usually served with honey?

56) What word means to steal livestock, especially cattle?

57) Who are the Pueblo Indians of Arizona?

58) Which community college is located on the Salt River Pima Indian Reservation?

59) What was the popular name of the predecessor of Interstate 40?

60) What are friendship tokens between the Hopi Indians and supernatural spirits?

61) How many Arizona dams are named for U.S. presidents?

62) Name Arizona's smallest Indian Reservation in land area.

63) What wood was made famous by Seri Indian woodcarvers?

64) What is the state gemstone?

65) What planet was known as Planet X?

66) What color is the star on Arizona's state flag?

67) Regarding unions and labor, what kind of state is Arizona?

68) What do Hawaii and Arizona have in common regarding the time of day?

69) What was the newspaper *The Arizona Republic* called prior to its current name?

70) For what mining product is Arizona number one in the nation?

71) When reading cattle brands, what is a letter lying on its side called?

72) Name the world famous medical organization that has a clinic in Scottsdale.

73) What did the call letters KTAR originally stand for?

74) What is the state tree of Arizona?

75) What is the word used to describe a spectacular strike of rich, high grade ore?

76) What famous Rough Rider is associated with the bronze statue in front of the Prescott courthouse?

77) Name the Indian tribe that performs the snake dance.

78) In a legal sense involving ownership, what kind of state is Arizona?

79) What is Arizona's number one job-producing industry?

80) What annual speech does the Governor of Arizona give on the second Monday of January?

81) What are Arizona's official colors?

82) According to *Ripley's Believe it or Not,* the tallest 3-story building in the world is: _____

83) What Arizona law enforcement agency celebrated its 25th anniversary in 1994?

84) Do Indian reservations comprise approximately 25%, 50%, or 75% of Arizona's land?

85) What elected county official has the duty to register voters in Arizona?

86) Name the car dealer magnate who made his mark by selling cars and trucks while atop a Brahma steer saying, "This ain't no bull!"

87) Is the Arizona legislature bicameral or unicameral?

88) What can be unusual about the time of day when one enters the Navajo Indian Reservation in Arizona?

89) How many red and yellow rays are on the Arizona state flag?

90) Name the World's largest horse-drawn parade.

91) Name this cartoonist who graduated from Phoenix Union High School just prior to World War II. In Europe, writing for *Stars and Stripes,* he created the grungy combat characters "Willie and Joe." The series, *"Up Front,"* was later made into a movie by the same name. He won two Pulitzer Prizes for his work.

92) Name the first full-blooded Native American to be appointed to West Point.

93) Which Arizona U.S. Senator was known as the "Father of the GI Bill?"

94) A 1995 winner of the Presidential Medal of Freedom, the nation's highest civilian award, is a former Phoenix resident (North Phoenix High School) Joan Ganz Cooney. She founded the Children's Television Workshop. Name the long-running television show that was her brainchild.

95) What was the site of Arizona's worst air crash?

96) What was Bethany Home Road in Phoenix named for?

97) What was the original name of these department stores: Robinson's-May, Dillards, Broadway-Southwest/Macy's.

98) Name two well-known Arizona newspapermen, historians and environmentalists, who died in 1996 in the same week.

99) Who coined the phrase about Scottsdale, "The West's Most Western Town"?

100) What range of mountains east of Phoenix are believed to be the hiding place of the Lost Dutchman mine?

Ernest W. McFarland—judge, senator, governor and member of the State Supreme Court.

(Photo courtesy Arizona Historical Society / Tucson)

General Trivia Answers

1) The Grand Canyon State
2) Climate, cotton, cattle, copper and citrus
3) Navajo
4) Tucson (Tucson—2,389 ft.; Phoenix—1,389 ft.)
5) Petrified Forest near Holbrook in Navajo County
6) The Navajo Nation
7) Katsina (Kachina) Dolls
8) Central Arizona Project (CAP)
9) Tequila
10) *Arizona Highways*
11) Bola tie
12) Monsoon season (July, August, September)
13) Fool's gold
14) Boot Hill (Tombstone)
15) Yavapai
16) State of Arizona
17) Old Main
18) Groundhog Day
19) Paolo Soleri
20) Mesquite
21) Holy Cross
22) Cotton
23) Arizona State University (Glendale & Tempe)
24) Kartchner Caverns
25) Presidio
26) Heard Museum
27) The Havasupai
28) Phoenix
29) Clovis Campbell, 1966
30) Liar (legend has it that after drinking from the Hassayampa River one can never tell the truth again)
31) A maternity ward
32) Adobe brick
33) Ditat Deus (God Enriches)
34) Secretary of State
35) To bring rain to sun-parched Hopi land
36) Apache
37) Prescott (1888)
38) February 14, 1912 (Valentine's Day)
39) Silversmithing
40) Navajo Community College at Tsaile, AZ (Navajo Reservation)
41) Unibomber. The FBI search lasted 18 years.
42) Kiva
43) Metate (ma-tah-tee)
44) Grand Canyon University
45) It was an earlyday racetrack on the outskirts of town.
46) Coolidge Dam
47) Four (red, blue, gold and copper)
48) Winged Victory
49) Copper
50) Luminaria (or farolito)
51) The Board of Regents
52) Pima cotton
53) Interstate 17
54) Dendrochronology
55) Sopaipilla (soap-a-pea-a)
56) Rustle
57) The Hopi
58) Scottsdale Community College
59) Route 66
60) Kachinas
61) Three (Roosevelt, Hoover and

Coolidge)

62) Tonto-Apache near Payson (85 acres)
63) Ironwood
64) Turquoise
65) Pluto (discovered in Flagstaff's Lowell Observatory)
66) Copper
67) Right-to-work state
68) They do not go on daylight-savings time
69) *The Arizona Republican*
70) Copper
71) Lazy
72) Mayo Clinic
73) Keep Taking the *Arizona Republican* (now known as *The Arizona Republic*)
74) Palo Verde
75) Bonanza
76) Buckey O'Neill
77) Hopi
78) Community property state
79) Tourism
80) State of the State address
81) Old gold and blue
82) Globe's Elks Club Building (high ceilings)
83) Department of Public Safety
84) 25% (actually 27%)
85) County Recorder

86) Tex Earnhardt
87) Bicameral
88) It goes on daylight-savings time and the rest of Arizona does not.
89) 13 (6 yellow/gold and 7 red)
90) Scottsdale's Parada Del Sol
91) Bill Mauldin
92) Emory Sekaquaptewa (Hopi)
93) Ernest W. McFarland
94) Sesame Street
95) Grand Canyon (128 people) 1956
96) The Bethany Home, an early-day tuberculosis sanitarium and goat farm at 16th St. and what is now Bethany Home Road.
97) Robinson's-May was Goldwater's and before that M. Goldwater and Bro. Dillard's was Diamond's (it originally opened as the Boston Store). Broadway-Southwest was formerly Korrick's and before that, the New York Store.
98) Ben Avery and Lester Ward "Budge" Ruffner.
99) Scottsdale artist Wes Segner (1946).
100) The Superstitions.

Katsina (Kachina) Dolls

A Historical Perspective

. . . a new state in an old land that is rich in history

This land we call Arizona was shaped by the rough hand of Mother Nature. It's an arid wilderness of brawny mountain ranges, rough-hewn mesas, sprawling rangelands and vast forests of cactus and trees. Its spectacular steep-sided canyons and picturesque salmon-hued buttes were carved over the ages by wind, sand and time. In the high country, twisting silver streams of clear mountain water glide through grassy meadows. The land is so diverse that scenic wonders existing in all the other forty-nine states can be found within its boundaries. A few years ago *Arizona Highways* ran a special issue called "Fifty in One." Photographers took pictures within this state showing scenic places found in each of the other forty-nine. That's diversity!

Arizona isn't only a contrast in geography; it's a land of many diverse cultures. Native Americans have lived here for thousands of years. Their tribal customs and languages differ much the same as the peoples of European nations. The Spanish explorers first entered this land in the mid-16th century, spreading their language and customs far and wide. Arizona was a part of Mexico until the mid-19th century.

America proudly boasts that it was a "melting pot" of races. Historically Arizona was more of a "mulligan stew." Here, Native American and Hispanic peoples didn't have an ocean separating them from their homeland; therefore, it has been relatively easy for them to maintain close ties with their ancestral homes. Theirs is a proud tradition and their ceremonies reflect this pride.

The "mulligan stew" label isn't as accurate today despite the fact that the Native American and Hispanic traditions are still strong. During the past 40 years the state population has grown from 850,000 to nearly 4 million. The great majority of these arrived from other states and have had a strong "melting pot" effect on the lifestyle and culture of Arizona.

The earliest inhabitants in what is now called Arizona were big game hunters, called Paleo-Indians. They arrived here at least 12,000 years ago. As the climate dried out and the big animals became extinct, they evolved into a desert style culture, living mostly on desert plants and small animals. About 4,000 years ago a group called the Cochise planted a primitive type of corn. Around the beginning of

 the Christian era, the Hohokam, Mogollon, Patayan and Anasazi emerged and lived here. Their cultures peaked around A.D. 1250 and were in decline by the 1400s.

By the time the Spanish arrived in the 1600s, others, including the Apache and Navajo, had taken up residence.

The first Spanish missionaries arrived in Arizona in 1629, settling among the Hopi Indians. They were driven out in the Great Pueblo Revolt in 1680 and never returned to the Hopi Mesas. During the 1690s, Father Eusebio Francisco Kino, the great Jesuit padre, made his entrance from the south, along the Santa Cruz River He established the Mission San Xavier del Bac near Tucson. Franciscan padres later established missions as far north as Tucson and as far west as Yuma. The Mission San Jose de Tumacacori is another fine example.

The earliest Anglo-Americans in Arizona were the fur trappers who came in the 1820s to trap for beaver. Legendary explorers and mountain men like Kit Carson, Joe Walker, Pauline Weaver, Antoine Leroux and Ewing Young rode the dangerous trails across Arizona during those years. They were a nomadic breed and left no tracks behind when they departed a decade later. The first American account of what Arizona was like during this time was published from the journal of a young mountain man named James Ohio Pattie who trapped the streams in 1826.

American soldiers crossed Arizona in 1846 during the war with Mexico but they, too, were only passing through. Arizona's lack of water and formidable deserts intimidated all but the most intrepid.

Following the 1848 Treaty of Guadalupe Hidalgo, ending the Mexican War, Arizona, then encompassing the areas north of the Gila River, became a part of the United States. In 1854, needing more suitable land to build a railroad to California the Gadsden Purchase was made which included all of the land south of the Gila to the present day border. Four years earlier, Arizona entered the Union as part of the New Mexico Territory. After a long struggle, the Arizonans secured a separate territory on February 24, 1863.

Since the days of the early Spanish explorers, Arizona had a wild and woolly reputation. The deserts were formidable and many of the natives intractable. The Spanish would concentrate most of their colonizing efforts in California and New Mexico. Arizona was the dreaded place a person had to cross to get from one to the other.

After Arizona became a U.S. territory its lands remained a refuge for Apache warriors who refused to accept reservation life and desperados who had been chased out of other states and territories. Notorious Apache leaders such as Geronimo and bloody feuds like that of the Earps and Clantons or the Grahams and Tewksburys presented Easterners with a perception that it was a lawless, uncivilized place not fit for statehood.

The discovery of gold and silver in the mountains of southern Arizona in the 1850s focused much attention on the area and marked the first major milestone in its history. Arizona became a territory in 1863 primarily because of its rich mineral resources.

The arrival of the railroads in the 1880s was the next great milestone for Arizona. Now people and much-needed supplies could be transported to and from the territory with relative ease. The Southern Pacific Railroad mainline reached Tucson in 1880 and Phoenix in 1926. A branch line from Maricopa linked Phoenix to the southern line in 1877. The Santa Fe Railroad mainline reached Flagstaff in 1881. In 1895 the Santa Fe completed the Ashfork-Prescott-Phoenix line, a date recognized as the "closing of the frontier" in Arizona history.

Water, or the lack of, continued to be a problem, especially in central Arizona where the community named Phoenix was built over the ashes of ancient Hohokam cities. The early irrigation ditches and canals dug hundreds of years ago by these prehistoric peoples delivered water to the fields of the farmers of the new community. Still, there wasn't enough water to serve a large population and during time of drought, there wasn't even enough to supply the existing population. That all changed in the early 1900s when Theodore Roosevelt Dam was built on the Salt River, another major milestone in the history of the state. It is a 13,000 sq. mile watershed in the central mountains, whose runoff is harnessed by several dams on the Salt and Verde Rivers ensuring the future water supplies of Salt River Valley residents.

Arizona enjoyed steady but relatively slow growth until World War II. The census of 1940 reported a population of less than 500,000 people. The population of Phoenix was 65,000. During the war the state became a veritable military training camp. The desert was an ideal training center for desert warfare and the clear skies allowed year around pilot training. Hundreds of thousands of soldiers and airmen became temporary residents as a result of the war and many returned. Arizona's modern history begins with this period.

Desert living in Arizona was made easier in the 1950s by the advent of affordable air conditioning. At that same time the relocation of several manufacturing companies to Arizona created more jobs. Success breeds success and since the 1950s more and more companies have moved here for a number of very good reasons. The Salt River Economic Report of 1990 listed the state's positive factors in this order:

1. Climate
2. Open spaces
3. Job opportunities
4. Lower living costs
5. Natural beauty
6. Friendliness of people
7. Abundance of natural resources
8. Minimum danger of physical hazards such as earthquakes or floods

Another study ranked the greater Phoenix area 10th in the nation on such factors as availability of labor, quality of life for employees, office and manufacturing facilities, office space, existing services and government climate. Still another ranked the area 8th thanks to excellent schools, well-educated work force and a large community college system able to support business needs. Companies relocating to Arizona find it easy to convince their employees to also make the move. People prefer the lifestyle in sun-kissed Arizona where year around outdoor and indoor recreation abounds. The N.B.A's Phoenix Suns were organized in 1968 and the N.F.L's Phoenix Cardinals moved here from St. Louis in 1988. Several Major League baseball teams train here in the spring. In 1995 the state was awarded a Major League baseball franchise. The Arizona Diamondbacks will begin play in 1998.

The National Hockey League's Winnipeg Jets moved their franchise to the America West Arena in 1995 (beginning play in the 1996-97 season) giving Arizona another Major League sport.

Magazines such as *Arizona Highways* highlighted the state's scenic beauty to people not only in the United States but throughout the world. Tourism became the leading job producer in Arizona, directly supporting nearly 100,000 jobs and indirectly supporting another 200,000.

Today some 18 million tourists a year visit the state, two million of whom are visitors from other countries. They spend approximately

$6 billion dollars annually.

In Arizona, there's something for everybody. Newcomers are always welcome because, as one put it, "nearly everyone else is a newcomer, too!"

Will Rogers said, "The Indians never got lost because they were always looking back over their shoulder to see where they'd been." Arizonans should always keep that sage advice in mind. We are a new place in an old land. The Indians respect the land because it is so old— the newcomers are in awe of the land because it is so new. History lives in Arizona—The past isn't dead—It isn't even past!

(above left) **Lorna Lockwood** of Douglas, AZ—the first woman to sit as Chief Justice of a State Supreme Court (AZ).

(above right) **Rose Mofford** of Globe, AZ—first woman governor of Arizona.

(left) **Justice Sandra Day O'Connor** of Duncan, AZ—first woman appointed to the U. S. Supreme Court.

Historical Trivia

1. Before Arizona became a territory in 1863, it was part of which territory?
2. From what observatory was the planet Pluto discovered?
3. From what city did Barry Goldwater launch his 1964 Presidential campaign?
4. What 1854 purchase of land from Mexico brought southern Arizona into the U.S.?
5. What former Arizona governor gave the Easter Sunrise Service at the Grand Canyon for 25 years?
6. Who was the first woman Governor of Arizona?
7. What historic Mormon fort is located in northwest Arizona?
8. What was the name given to the U.S. Cavalry's black soldiers?
9. Who did Barry Goldwater defeat for the United States Senate in 1952 in one of Arizona's major political upsets?
10. What institution used the slogan "Arizona grows where water flows"?
11. Who is credited with having given Phoenix its name?

Barry Goldwater at the Prescott Frontier Days parade in 1964.

(Photo courtesy Sharlot Hall Museum)

12. What happened on October 26, 1881 in Tombstone that brought everlasting fame to Wyatt Earp?

13. What were the General Jessup and Nina Tilden?

14. Who headed the Spanish expedition comprised of the first non-Indians to see the Grand Canyon?

15. Which of the Earp brothers was gunned down in Hatch's Saloon (in Tombstone) in 1882?

16. What person is credited with introducing cattle to Arizona?

17. What well-known Arizona resort was established by Isabella Greenway?

18. What is Tombstone's most famous newspaper?

19. Who was President of the United States when Arizona became a state?

20. What ethnic group provided most of the labor for southern Arizona's first railroad?

21. Name one of Arizona's four original counties.

22. Who was the State of Arizona's first congressman?

23. What notorious Arizona group of strikers agitated against capitalistic enterprises such as copper mining?

24. In 1909, the Arizona territorial prison moved from where to where?

25. Which former Arizona politician was a major contender for the United States presidential nomination in 1976?

26. What was the first Indian reservation in Arizona?

27. Which U.S. Senator from Arizona was called the "showhorse" because of his great speechmaking ability?

28. What Indian tribe name means "The Peaceful People"?

29. Name the tunnel used by German POWs for their daring "great escape" at Papago Park in Phoenix.

30. What silver-tongued orator and Presidential candidate spoke in Phoenix on statehood day in 1912?

31. Who headed the largest Spanish exploration through Arizona in 1540?

32. Arizona was a part of what country before it was a part of the U.S.?

33. Name the former Arizona governor known as "The Pathfinder".

34. What Arizona law enforcement group was formed in 1901 mostly to resist the rustler element in Arizona?

35. Name the United States' largest World War II heavy-bomber training base.

36. Name the House minority leader who retired in 1982 after 30 years in the U.S. Congress.

37. What were the Tohono O'odham Indians formerly called?

38. What was Arizona's most famous silver boomtown?

39. What famous Apache Chief had a stronghold in the Dragoon Mountains?

40. Who was Arizona's first woman member of Congress?

41. What was the primary purpose for which the Salt River Project was established?

42. Who was Arizona's first Mexican-American governor?

43. What was the more popular name of the Aztec Land & Cattle Company in the 1890s?

44. What were Salado and Patayan?

45. What Phoenix area school was first known as the "Normal School?"

46. Who starred at the St. Louis World's Fair, rode in Teddy Roosevelt's inaugural parade, and died at Fort Sill, Oklahoma in 1909?

47. Who was Arizona's Mormon "Buckskin Missionary" in the 1890s?

48. Who made the nominating speech for Barry Goldwater in 1964?

49. Where in Arizona is one of the two bells from the battleship USS Arizona?

50. What Arizona city started a free-milk-at-lunch program in 1933 that was later implemented nationally?

51. Where did the first steam locomotive enter Arizona?

52. What communication system, used in Arizona by the U.S.

Cavalry, uses mirrors to send messages?

53. In what town did New York Mayor Fiorello La Guardia spend his boyhood years?

54. What is the greatest single naval loss in U.S. history?

55. Name the architect of Grady Gammage Auditorium at ASU?

56. In what year did Arizona become a territory?

57. Whose political career was launched in 1949 with the election to the Phoenix City Council on the reform ticket?

58. Which Attorney General admitted to a lifelong love affair with the search for the fabled Lost Dutchman Gold Mine?

59. What discovery in Arizona was a leading reason for the creation of the Arizona Territory by Congress?

60. Who was William Bonney better known as?

61. What was the only walled U.S. city during the mid-19th century?

62. What was known as a Concord in Arizona?

63. When did Arizona have a government but no votes in Congress?

64. What popular radio personality became Mayor of Phoenix and closed his political career as Governor of Arizona?

65. What Catholic religious order built missions among the Hopi Indians in the 1900s?

66. Who dedicated Tucson's Davis-Monthan airport?

67. Name three Arizona cities that have been both a county seat and the capital of Arizona.

68. What person has the distinct honor of representing Arizona as Governor, U.S. Senator and Chief Justice of the Arizona Supreme Court?

69. What city was the backdrop for the movie "The Great White Hope"?

70. Why is Arizona known as the nation's valentine?

71. What Arizona community took its name from a mining magnate and state senator who built it for his employees?

72. Name the first United States President to visit Arizona.

73. Who was the first Arizonan to serve in a United States

President's cabinet?

74. For what is J.C. Adams best remembered in Arizona?

75. What was the river crossing near the Tempe bridge once called?

76. Which U.S. President signed the law creating the Arizona Territory?

77. Who discovered the Vulture Mine?

78. Who did Will Rogers call "Arizona's perennial governor"?

79. What does the CO in Babbitt's historic CO Bar Ranch stand for?

80. Who was Arizona's first governor to actually serve in the Arizona Territory?

81. Whose personal narrative diary served as one of the first books on the Southwest?

82. Name one of two "Miss Americas" from Arizona.

83. Who is Cara Jackson?

84. What trailblazer had a mountain, a stream and a town named after him?

85. In 1781, what Franciscan missionary was murdered during an uprising at Yuma?

86. Name the Pulitzer Prize-winning cartoonist who entertained readers of *The Arizona Republic* for three generations.

87. What 1966 event in the Arizona legislature changed the face of Arizona politics forever?

88. When is Mexico's Independence Day? (From Spain)

89. What woman broke a 190-year-old male legal tradition?

90. What famous western artist spent his formative years in frontier Arizona with the U.S. Cavalry?

91. Who is Arizona's best-known woman stagecoach robber?

92. What notorious Yuma institution closed in 1909?

93. Name the medical officer who served on the Arizona frontier where he first began his studies on malaria and yellow fever.

94. What did the Enabling Act, passed by Congress in 1910, do?

95. What famous WWII General trained desert troops in southwest Arizona?

96. What Apache leader's real name was "Go Khla Yeh" (he who yawns)?

97. Which United States battleship, sunk at Pearl Harbor on December 7, 1941, is still commissioned?

98. What was Dr. John Holliday's better known occupation?

99. Who did Morris Udall replace in Congress from District 2 in 1961?

100. Who were the major prehistoric cliff dwellers of the Four Corners region?

101. What was the leading industry in the Salt River Valley during World War I?

102. Name the only Arizona governor to be impeached.

103. What was Papago Park in Phoenix used for in the 1940s?

104. Name one of two Arizona governors to die in office.

105. For how many years was Tucson the capital of Arizona?

106. In what decade was Hoover Dam started and completed?

107. What was the "Lost Dutchman's" name?

108. Name the brothers who took the first motion pictures of the Grand Canyon.

109. What were the mysterious cities of gold called by the Spaniards?

110. Name Tombstone's famous photographer who was later a sheriff of Cochise County.

111. Who was Arizona governor immediately preceding Rose Mofford?

112. Of whom are Arizona's two authorized statues in Statuary Hall in the Capitol rotunda in Washington, D.C.?

113. What group of people dug the Mesa Canal and established a farming community in the 1890s?

114. What was James Addison Reavis better known as?

115. How many legislative districts does Arizona have?

116. Who operated a ferry on the upper Colorado near Page until his execution by a firing squad?

117. What Arizonan served longer in the U.S. Congress than

any other American?

118. From whom did the Apache Indians get their first horses?

119. When told all Arizona needed to make it a decent place was a few good people and water, what famous general replied, "That's all hell needs!"?

120. What was the original name of Seligman?

121. What great institution sits on land donated by a saloonkeeper and two gamblers?

122. In what town did the famous "six gun classic" shootout occur between Joe Phy and Pete Gabriel?

123. What Spanish soldier blazed an overland trail to California in 1774?

124. With which territory did Arizona have a "joint statehood" bill proposed in the early 1900s?

125. Name the treaty that gave all of Arizona north of the Gila River to the United States after the Mexican War.

126. What did Esther Ross do with a bottle of water from the spillway of the first water opening of Roosevelt Dam?

127. Name the long-haired Apache County Sheriff who had a classic shootout in Holbrook in 1887.

128. What did Arizonans Port Parker and Everett Bowman do in London in 1934?

129. Who was Arizona's first Hispanic state senate majority leader?

130. Name the famous scout who guided General Kearny's Army of the West across Arizona (Mexican War).

131. What newspaper columnist and author was instrumental in organizing the Dons Club and wrote a best seller on the Lost Dutchman Gold Mine?

132. Which Arizona city started as a Spanish presidio or fort in 1775?

133. Who was the first woman to serve as Chief Justice of any state supreme court?

134. What was Arizona's most famous U.S. mail stagecoach line?

135. What was the first resort in the Salt River Valley?

136. What common term described the gold seekers who crossed Arizona on their way to California?

137. Who developed Sun City?

138. Who was Tombstone's "gunshot physician?"

139. In 1924, when Tucson residents saw "Shenandoah", what did they see?

140. Who was Prescott's "First Citizen?"

141. Who was the first woman to serve on the Navajo Tribal Council?

142. What famous theater's name was inspired by the song *She Was Only a Bird in a Gilded Cage?*

143. Who was the last major Apache leader to surrender to the United States Army?

144. Who was most responsible for restoring Prescott's Territorial governor's mansion and converting it to a museum?

145. Who was "blood brother" to Cochise?

146. Who was Arizona's "trunk murderess"?

147. Who designed the Arizona Biltmore Hotel?

148. Who led the first complete exploration of the Grand Canyon?

149. Name a former United States Vice President who had his winter home in Scottsdale and whose famous saying was, "What this country needs is a good 5-cent cigar."

150. Who was president of both Arizona State Teacher's College at Flagstaff and Arizona State University?

151. What was the Honeymoon Trail?

152. Who was Howard Pyle's manager in the 1950 gubernatorial campaign?

153. Who was the only woman sheriff in Maricopa County?

154. Why was former Arizona Governor Hunt called George VII?

155. The Globe and Northern Railroad's Loco #1 original name was "Jupiter". Where did this little locomotive carve its niche in history?

156. What famous explorer was also a governor of Arizona?

157. What historic event took place in Nogales on June 6, 1936?

158. Name the judge who presided over the Evan Mecham

impeachment trial in 1988.

159. Who was the first African-American U.S. Marshal in Arizona?

160. Name the fire that destroyed Zane Grey's Cabin in 1990.

161. Name the first woman Mayor of Phoenix.

162. Name the first Hispanic elected official in Phoenix.

163. Name the prehistoric settlers in the Phoenix area that engineered what was then the world's most extensive irrigation canal system.

164. Who was the first Asian-American elected mayor of a major U.S. city?

165. How many counties did Arizona have when it became a state?

166. Who was Arizona's "Balloon Buster" in World War I and the first aviator to win the Congressional Medal of Honor?

167. Who was the only Arizonan to win the Congressional Medal of Honor during World War II?

168. Who ran for governor against Bruce Babbitt in 1978?

169. Where was the "granddaddy" of all silver strikes in Arizona?

170. What was the first official territorial capital of Arizona?

171. What Arizona city is known as the "Old Pueblo"?

172. Name the most famous Indian hero of World War II who is in the famous photograph of Iwo Jima.

173. Name the former Governor of Arizona who has been a United States Ambassador to 3 countries.

174. Name the former riverport city that was also home of Arizona's infamous territorial prison.

175. Name the two religious orders of Catholic missionaries who came to Arizona in the 1600s.

176. How many "Arizonan" crew members perished on the USS Arizona?

177. What was the name of the Marines' Navajo communications troops during WWII?

178. In what decade did work commence on Roosevelt Dam?

179. Name two federal work programs conducted in Arizona during the 1930s Depression.

180. For what are Jack Burden and Romaine Lowdermilk of Wickenburg best remembered?

181. Where was the battleship USS Arizona sunk?

182. Who was the "Father of the Democratic Party" in Arizona?

183. Name the first Arizonan inducted into the National Cowboy Hall of Fame.

184. Who is regarded as the Father of Arizona?

185. What was the nickname of Arizona National Guard's 158th Infantry regiment during World War II?

186. In what year did Arizona become a state?

187. What is Arizona's most celebrated 1963 criminal court case?

188. What famous gunfighter/sheriff once owned the San Bernardino Ranch near Douglas?

189. Was Arizona the 47th, 48th or 49th state admitted to the Union?

190. Name the California-bound family that was massacred near Gila Bend in 1851.

191. What Indians are known as the "Cowboy Indians?"

192. Who was Mexico's infamous border raider?

193. Who was the first woman elected majority leader of a state senate?

194. Name the head of the historic grocery chain family who ran for governor of Arizona in 1994.

195. Name this famous Arizona outdoor and political newspaper writer. A shooting range off I-17 north of Phoenix was named in his honor.

196. What did Frank Luke, Ira H. Hayes and Silvestre Herrera have in common?

Frank Luke—WW I fighter ace

Ira Hayes—Pima Indian, hero of famous flag-raising photograph on Iwo Jima in World War II.
(Photo courtesy Arizona State Library)

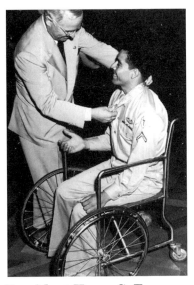
President Harry S. Truman congratulates Army P.F.C. ***Silvestre Herrera***—the only Arizonan to win the Medal of Honor in World War II.
(Photo courtesy Arizona Hall of Fame)

Historical Trivia Answers

1. New Mexico Territory
2. Lowell Observatory (Flagstaff)
3. Prescott (on the courthouse steps)
4. Gadsden Purchase
5. Howard Pyle (1935-1960)
6. Rose Mofford (1988-1991)
7. Pipe Spring (National Monument)
8. Buffalo Soldiers (formed in 1866)
9. Ernest W. McFarland
10. Salt River Project
11. Darrell Duppa (Jack Swilling also acceptable)
12. The Gunfight at OK Corral
13. Arizona steamboats
14. Captain Garciá López de Cárdenas
15. Morgan
16. Father Kino (1691-1711)
17. The Arizona Inn, Tucson
18. *The Tombstone Epitaph*
19. William Howard Taft
20. The Chinese
21. Pima, Yuma, Yavapai and Mohave
22. Carl Hayden
23. The Wobblies (Industrial Workers of the World, I.W.W.), 1917
24. Yuma to Florence
25. Morris "Mo" Udall
26. Gila Reservation (Pima Indians)
27. Henry Fountain Ashurst (1912-1941)
28. Hopi
29. Faustball Tunnel (1944)
30. William Jennings Bryan
31. Francisco Vasquez de Coronado
32. Mexico
33. John C. Fremont (1878-1882)
34. The Arizona Rangers
35. Davis-Monthan (Tucson)
36. John J. Rhodes
37. Papago
38. Tombstone
39. Cochise (Cochise Stronghold)
40. Isabella S. Greenway (1933-1937)
41. To finance construction of Roosevelt Dam (1911)
42. Raul Castro (1975-1977)
43. Hashknife
44. Prehistoric Indian tribes
45. Arizona State University
46. Geronimo
47. Jacob Hamblin
48. Ronald Reagan
49. Student Union Belltower, University of Arizona (the other is at Pearl Harbor)
50. Florence
51. Yuma, 1877
52. Heliograph system
53. Prescott
54. Sinking of the USS Arizona (1,177 men)
55. Frank Lloyd Wright
56. 1863
57. Barry Goldwater
58. Bob Corbin
59. Gold was discovered
60. Billy the Kid
61. Tucson (Presidio of Tucson)
62. A stagecoach
63. When it was a Territory (1863-1912)
64 Jack Williams (Mayor—

1956-1960, Governor 1967-1975)
65. Franciscans
66. Charles Lindbergh (1927)
67. Phoenix, Tucson and Prescott
68. Ernest W. McFarland
69. Globe
70. It was admitted to statehood on Valentine's Day.
71. Clarkdale (William A. Clark)
72. William McKinley, 1901
73. Stewart Udall, Secretary of the Interior under John F. Kennedy (1961)
74. He built the Adams Hotel (Phoenix)
75. Hayden's Ferry
76. Abraham Lincoln
77. Henry Wickenburg
78. George Hunt (seven terms)
79. Cincinnati, Ohio. (Prior hometown of the five Babbitt Brothers who arrived in Arizona in the 1880s)
80. John N. Goodwin
81. James Ohio Pattie (1826)
82. Jacque Mercer, 1949, and Vonda Kay Van Dyke, 1964
83. The first African-American Miss Arizona (1995)
84. Bill Williams (Mountain Man)
85. Frey Garcés
86. Reg Manning
87. Reapportionment, (one person - one vote)
88. September 16
89. Sandra Day O'Connor, U.S. Supreme Court Justice from Arizona. (Appointed 1981)
90. Frederic Remington
91. Pearl Hart
92. Yuma Territorial Prison
93. Dr. Walter Reed (1875)
94. Allowed Arizonans to prepare for statehood by writing a state constitution
95. General George Patton
96. Geronimo
97. USS Arizona
98. Professional gambler (or gunslinger)
99. Stewart Udall (his brother)
100. Anasazi Indians
101. Cotton growing
102. Evan Mecham (1988)
103. Prisoner of War camp
104. Sidney P. Osborn (1948) and Wesley Bolin (1978)
105. Ten (1867 - 1877)
106. 1930s (1931-1936)
107. Jacob Waltz
108. Emery and Ellsworth Kolb
109. Seven Cities of Cibola
110. C.S. Fly (Camillus S. Fly)
111. Evan Mecham
112. Father Kino and John Greenway
113. Mormon colonists from Utah
114. The Baron of Arizona. He tried to swindle the government out of nearly 12 million acres on a phony Spanish land grant.
115. Thirty
116. John Doyle Lee (1877)
117. Carl Hayden (1912-1969)
118. Spaniards
119. General William T. Sherman during a summer visit in the 1880s
120. Prescott Junction
121. University of Arizona
122. Florence (1888)
123. Captain Juan Bautista de Anza
124. New Mexico

125. Treaty of Guadalupe Hidalgo (1848)
126. Christened the USS Arizona (June 19, 1915)
127. Commodore Perry Owens
128. Gave a command rodeo performance
129. Alfredo Gutierrez
130. Kit Carson (1846)
131. Oren Arnold
132. Tucson
133. Lorna Lockwood (Arizona) (1965)
134. Butterfield Overland Mail
135. Ingleside Inn (1909)
136. Forty-niners
137. Del E. Webb
138. Dr. George Goodfellow
139. A blimp
140. Pauline Weaver, earlyday trapper and army scout
141. Anne Dodge Wauneka (elected 1951—served 5 terms)
142. Bird Cage Theater (Tombstone)
143. Geronimo (1886)
144. Sharlot Hall
145. Tom Jeffords
146. Winnie Ruth Judd
147. Albert Chase McArthur (Frank Lloyd Wright was a consultant)
148. Major John Wesley Powell (1869)
149. Thomas R. Marshall (Vice President two terms under Woodrow Wilson)
150. Grady Gammage—Arizona State Teacher's College (NAU) (1926-1933), Arizona State University (1933-1959)
151. Road from Winslow to St. George, Utah. Prior to 1926, Mormon couples had to travel to the Mormon Temple in Utah to be married.
152. Barry Goldwater
153. Jewel Jordan (In 1944 she succeeded her husband who died in office.)
154. He was elected Governor seven times.
155. It participated in the golden spike ceremony linking transcontinental railroad in 1869 at Promontory Point, Utah
156. John C. Fremont, "The Great Pathfinder", was governor from 1878 to 1882.
157. The first barrel of tequila made in the U.S. was produced at the San Andres distillery.
158. Frank X. Gordon (Chief Justice of the State Supreme Court)
159. Lee Limbs, appointed in 1976
160. The Dude
161. Margaret Hance (1975-1983)
162. Town Marshal Henry Garfias, May 3, 1891
163. Hohokam Indians
164. Willie Wong, Mesa, 1991
165. Fourteen
166. Frank Luke
167. Silvestre Herrera
168. Evan Mecham
169. Tombstone, 1877
170. Prescott (1864)
171. Tucson
172. Ira H. Hayes, Pima Indian
173. Raul Castro (El Salvador, Bolivia and Argentina)

174. Yuma
175. Jesuits and Franciscans
176. Seven
177. Code Talkers: Navajo men sent messages in Navajo code which the Japanese never could understand.
178. 1900 (1906-1911)
179. WPA, PWA, NYA, CCC
180. Founded the first dude ranches there (1920s)
181. Pearl Harbor, December 7, 1941
182. Morris Goldwater (Barry Goldwater's uncle)
183. George Ruffner, Yavapai County Sheriff (1893-1933)
184. Charles D. Poston
185. Bushmasters
186. 1912 (February 14)
187. The Miranda case (reading of rights)
188. John Slaughter
189. 48th
190. Oatman (3 Oatman children survived the massacre)
191. Apaches
192. Pancho Villa
193. Sandra Day O'Connor (AZ)
194. Eddie Basha
195. Ben Avery
196. All were war heroes from Arizona.

Jacque Mercer—Arizona's first Miss America

Lincoln Ragsdale—one of the Tuskeegee Airmen, the elite group of African-Americans to fly in action in the 99th Group in WWII.

(Photo courtesy the Ragsdale family)

Geography of Arizona

An automobile trip from Tucson to the top of the nearby Santa Catalina Mountains takes less than an hour yet the life zones traversed are equal to a trip from the southern border of the United States to Canada.

The December 1983 issue of *Arizona Highways* took its readers on a photo tour of the nation illustrating the scenic wonders one might see while visiting each of the fifty states. At first, one might ask, "Why is the magazine promoting the beauty of *other* states?" Truth is, all the photographs were shot within the boundaries of Arizona. They titled the issue appropriately, "Fifty in One."

Arizona is nestled in a magical arena of scenic geography. It is an extension of the great western mountain ranges—the Rockies, Sierra Nevada and the Sierra Madre. The Colorado Plateau stretches down across much of the northern part of the state. Here lie the spectacular salmon-hued canyons, buttes, mesas and spires of Canyon de Chelly and Monument Valley. The state's tallest mountains, the San Francisco Peaks, are also on the plateau as is that humongous gully, the Grand Canyon. There are mountains of all ages, shapes and origins. Rainfall varies from 3 inches annually in the low deserts to 30 in the high country. Often, the state records both the nation's high and low on the same day.

Several deserts overlap the state, including the Great Basin, Mojave, Chihuahuan, and of course, the beautiful Sonoran. The state tree is the paloverde and the state flower is the blossom of the majestic saguaro cactus. The grasslands, deserts and mountains also pull in their respective biotic species. People come from all over the globe to study and enjoy the geographic, geological and biotic life in Arizona. All seven of the Merriam Life Zones can be found in Arizona.

Generally, Arizona slopes towards the southwest. With the exception of the San Simon, San Pedro, Santa Cruz and Little Colorado, all the rivers flow south or west. And, those four rivers flow into rivers that flow south or west. Water, anywhere in the state, flowing unimpeded would wind up in Yuma sooner or later.

The rugged mountains above the Salt River Valley provide a 13,000 square-mile watershed for the residents. The building of dams on the Salt and Verde rivers during the early part of the 20th Century virtually assured the future growth of the Salt River Valley and guaranteed a reliable source of water.

Arizona can be divided into three physiographic zones. The three zones are roughly equal in size. The **Plateau Zone** is the largest, covering 42% of the state, followed by the **Desert** (or Basin and Range) **Zone** with 30%. The remaining 28% is in the **Mountain Zone.**

And, there are many contrasts within those zones. For example, in the spectacular wind-eroded, reddish-hued sandstone cliffs, buttes and spires of the **Plateau Zone,** one also finds lush forests and cool mountain streams in the Chuska Mountains above Canyon de Chelly; the high, wide and lonesome Arizona Strip country contrasts sharply with the lofty green-forested Kaibab Plateau. Both are flanked by the awesome North Rim of the mighty Grand Canyon.

The late Reg Manning, a Pulitzer Prize-winning cartoonist, who wrote several wonderful books on Arizona cacti said: "If you were a giant and wanted to eat the state of Arizona, you would find that roughly it would take three large and widely different mouthfuls."

The Plateau is a giant, uplifted land mass that extends into Colorado, New Mexico and Utah. It makes up the northern third and includes the White Mountains, Painted Desert, Petrified Forest, Grand Canyon, Monument Valley, Canyon de Chelly, Arizona Strip, Kaibab Plateau, San Francisco Mountains, Black Mesa, (including the Hopi Mesas) and the high country that borders the Mogollon (pronounced muggy-on) Rim. It ranges from 4,000 feet all the way to the top of Humphreys Peak in the San Francisco Mountains, the highest point in the state at 12,633 feet above sea level.

The contrasts are startling—near the wind-sculpted spires and buttes, mesas and steep-sided sandstone canyons of the Colorado Plateau are found lush forests with cool mountain streams in the Chuska Mountains.

The region also boasts the world's largest stand of ponderosa pine. It is best described as high, wide and handsome—a geographic collection of spectacular scenery and diversity that can't be matched anywhere else in the world.

The **Desert Zone** (or Basin and Range), which covers the western edge and the entire southern one-third of the state is a zone that actually extends from New Mexico, on the east, south into Mexico, west to the Sierra Nevada and northward into Oregon and Idaho. This zone can be divided into four sections that are generally identified by climate and vegetation. They are the Mexican Highlands, in the southeast corner of the state; the Gila Semi-desert in the central and southern. This includes the area around Phoenix and Tucson. The Colorado Desert occupies the southwest corner; and the Mojave Desert is in the west-center along the Colorado River.

The Basin and Range Zone is characterized by rugged mountains separated by broad, flat valleys. There are more than 150 mountain ranges. All were formed the same way and are essentially alike although they do vary in age. Many are rich in minerals. Much of the state's mineral wealth came from these irregular, rough-hewn mountain ranges. Tales of gold and silver from these mountains tickled the fancy of many a would-be millionaire. Old-timers used to say, "if ya stumble on a rock, don't cuss it, cash it." and "if ya wash yer face in the Hassayampa River, you can pan 4 ounces of gold dust from your whiskers."

The Basin and Range Zone has islands of mountains including the Santa Ritas, Catalinas, Chiricahuas, Pinal, Galiuro, Dragoons and Pinalenos. Mount Graham in the Pinalenos is nearly 11,000 feet in elevation and is the highest mountain in southern Arizona. The rolling, grass-carpeted and oak studded hills of Santa Cruz county are a startling contrast to the deserts between Nogales and Yuma. About 90% of Arizona's population resides in the Basin and Range Zone.

The **Mountain Zone** is a transition between the Plateau and the Basin and Range. This area is characterized by rugged, brawny mountains that aren't noted for their lofty heights whose ranges, in many cases, blend into one another. In other places, such as the upper Verde Valley and Tonto Basin, broad valleys separate the mountain ranges. The rocks run the geological gamut—sedimentary, metamorphic and volcanic. Some of the mountains, such as the Bradshaws, in Yavapai County, are highly mineralized. The Mountain Zone also includes the Mazatzal and Sierra Anchas which, along with the Bradshaws, provide an important watershed for the Salt River Valley and the lower Gila Valley.

Geography Trivia

1. Name one of three Arizona dams named after U.S. Presidents.
2. What mountain range is north of Tucson?
3. What Indian reservation is located completely within the boundaries of another?
4. The historic Q Ranch in bordering Pleasant Valley (Young, AZ) is in the area of which two feuding families?
5. What is Arizona's longest river?
6. Within 25 miles, how long is the Grand Canyon?
7. Name the highest mountain peak in Arizona.
8. Which rim of the Grand Canyon is higher, the north or south rim?
9. What city is located near Lynx Lake?
10. What northern Arizona mountain range was named by early Spanish missionaries for their patron Saint?
11. On what Indian reservation is Kitt Peak Observatory located?
12. Compared to all the states, does Arizona rank third, fourth, sixth or ninth in terms of land area?
13. What is Arizona's largest state park?
14. Which city is highest in elevation: Nogales or Bisbee?
15. What east-west interstate highway replaced Route 66 across northern Arizona?
16. What peaks grace Flagstaff?
17. Where are the Granite Dells?
18. Name Arizona's largest land owner.
19. What lake is behind Hoover Dam?
20. In what county is Tombstone located?
21. How many counties are there in Arizona?
22. What two communities make up the Round Valley?
23. What lake is behind Coolidge Dam?
24. What Arizona county derives its name from an Indian tribe name meaning Sun People?
25. Name the breathtaking pass atop the Tucson Mountains.

26. Name 3 states (U.S.) that border Arizona.

27. What is the so-called "Backbone of Arizona Geography"?

28. In what county are the Superstition Mountains located?

29. What community north of Phoenix, perched on the side of a creek, takes its name from nearby caves?

30. What is the name of Phoenix's dromedary-shaped mountain?

31. What county takes its name from a high mountain located within its boundaries?

32. What lake is behind Horse Mesa Dam?

33. Where are Arizona's only native palm trees located?

34. What dam located southeast of Globe is named after a U.S. President?

35. What geographical part of Arizona is named for Juan Ignacio Flores Mogollon?

36. Near what city is the lowest point in Arizona?

37. What is the second-largest county in the United States in terms of land area?

38. Name the Arizona town that has the same name as one of the Great Lakes.

39. Name one of the three highest San Francisco peaks.

40. In what mountain range is Sabino Canyon located?

41. Name the highest mountain peak that towers above the White Mountains.

42. What county can boast over 1,000 miles of shoreline?

43. In what county is Tucson located?

44. Which of the world's seven natural wonders is in Arizona?

45. With what city is Thumb Butte associated?

46. Near what mountains is the Lost Frenchman Mine?

47. What site is commonly referred to as "the other national park in Arizona"?

48. Name an Arizona county that does not have an Indian reservation.

49. In what mountain range is beautiful Madera Canyon located?

50. Name the Mexican state that borders Arizona.

51. Where does the water from the Colorado River empty?

52. What hilly town introduced coaster racing to the nation in 1911?

53. What dam has Lake Mohave behind it?

54. Name northern Arizona's best known and most recent volcano.

55. Name the county seat of Greenlee County.

56. Name the states that touch Arizona at the four corners.

57. What Arizona city has California to the north and Mexico to the west?

58. Name one of the three mountains at Sunrise Ski Area.

59. What is the Mexican city next to Douglas?

60. Name two of the three towns on Cochise County's "Ghost Town Trail".

61. What county is known as the "mother of counties" and had 4 counties and parts of 5 other counties carved from it?

62. What was Hoover Dam first called?

63. How many Arizona counties are bigger than the state of Rhode Island?

64. What river is also known as "Big Red"?

65. What Arizona city, with a population of approximately 7,000, is named after a U.S. President?

66. Name the river that cuts a swath through the bottom of the Grand Canyon?

67. The Four Peaks are located in what mountain range?

68. Near what city is Arizona's highest peak, Humphreys Peak?

69. What Arizona county is larger than New Hampshire, Delaware and New Jersey combined?

70. What interstate highway connects Phoenix and Tucson?

71. What city takes its name from a mythical bird that burned itself in a funeral pyre and rose from its ashes?

72. Within 50 miles, how long is Arizona (maximum) from north-to-south and east-to-west?

73. What city is the Vulture Mine near?

74. Fort Whipple is near what city?

75. What is the county seat of La Paz county?

76. What is Arizona's newest county?

77. What Arizona city was formerly known as Hayden and Zeno?

78. What is Arizona's largest wet, or dry, natural lake?

79. In what county is McNary?

80. Into what river do all other rivers in Arizona eventually flow?

81. Pirtleville is a suburb of what city?

82. What is the name used to describe State Route 87 connecting Mesa and Scottsdale with Payson?

83. What is the common name for the old Highway 666 (now Highway 191) that runs from Clifton to Alpine?

84. What is the better known name for Arizona Route 88?

85. Name one river that flows north from Mexico and joins the Gila River.

86. Name Arizona's smallest county.

87. Near what Arizona city would one find Becker Lake and Becker Creek?

88. What national forest in Arizona is named after a Spanish explorer?

89. Name central Arizona's four "chain" lakes.

90. How many dams are located on the Colorado River?

91. Name the second highest peak in Arizona.

92. In what National Forest are the Santa Catalina Mountains?

93. One of the world's largest pine forests is found in Arizona. Name the species of pine.

94. What is the largest Indian reservation in Arizona?

95. What Arizona body of water was named after the 26th president of the U.S.?

96. Name the large body of water due south of Yuma.

97. In what county is Alpine, Arizona located?

98. Name the "Parkway" that runs from Oracle Junction to Florence.

99. What Arizona mountain range takes its name from th "King of Arizona" mine?

100. Name the towering peak in the Santa Rita Mountains south of Tucson.

101. Name the picturesque mountains east of Tombstone.

102. Name the one place (and the states) in the United States where four states meet.

103. What is the area of land north of the Grand Canyon in the northwest corner of Arizona called?

104. How many states does Arizona border?

105. What northern Arizona highway had a TV show named after it?

106. What is the only Arizona county named for an Indian leader?

107. What is the lake behind Glen Canyon Dam?

108. At what intersection in Phoenix do all addresses originate, Point 0?

109. What military post is now buried beneath the waters of Lake Mohave?

110. What Interstate runs from Gila Bend to San Diego?

111. What is the southernmost snow-skiing area in North America?

112. What famous valley is on the Navajo Reservation?

113. What is the name of Arizona's so-called "Lost County"?

114. What river crosses southern Arizona from New Mexico to Yuma?

115. What lake is behind Parker Dam?

116. Where in Arizona is the Camino del Diablo or Devil's Highway?

117. Name the mountain range that towers above the old town of Tubac.

118. What national monument is perched on the cliffs above Roosevelt Lake?

119. What national monument began as a fortress for early Mormon colonizers?

120. What is the only Arizona river that originates in Mexico?

Geography Trivia Answers

1. Roosevelt, Coolidge, and Hoover Dam
2. Santa Catalina Mountains
3. Hopi (surrounded by the Navajo Reservation)
4. Grahams and Tewksburys
5. The Colorado. Total length of the Colorado is 1,440 mi. of which 688 are in Arizona (277 mi. are in the Grand Canyon).
6. 277 miles
7. Humphrey's Peak, Flagstaff (12,633 feet)
8. North rim (1200 feet higher) Point Imperial is the highest point at 8872 feet.
9. Prescott
10. San Francisco Peaks (St. Francis of Assisi)
11. Papago (Tohono O'odham)
12. Sixth
13. Lake Havasu State Park
14. Bisbee (5,000 feet)
15. Interstate 40
16. San Francisco Peaks
17. Prescott
18. Federal Government
19. Lake Mead
20. Cochise County
21. 15
22. Springerville and Eagar
23. San Carlos Lake
24. Yavapai
25. Gates Pass
26. California, Nevada, Utah, Colorado, and New Mexico
27. Mogollon Rim
28. Pinal
29. Cave Creek
30. Camelback Mountain
31. Graham (Mt. Graham)
32. Apache Lake
33. Palm Canyon, Kofa Mountain Range
34. Coolidge Dam
35. Mogollon Rim
36. Yuma area (approximately 137 feet)
37. Coconino (San Bernardino, CA is the largest)
38. Superior
39. Humphrey's Peak, 12,633'; Mt. Agassiz, 12,356'; and Fremont Peak, 11,940'
40. Santa Catalina Mountains
41. Mount Baldy
42. Mohave
43. Pima
44. Grand Canyon
45. Prescott
46. Eagletail Mountains
47. Petrified Forest National Park
48. Cochise, Greenlee or Santa Cruz
49. Santa Rita Mountains
50. Sonora
51. Sea of Cortez (Gulf of California)
52. Bisbee
53. Davis Dam
54. Sunset Crater (A.D. 1064-65)
55. Clifton
56. Utah, Colorado, and New Mexico
57. Yuma
58. Apache Peak, Cyclone Circle and Sunrise Peak
59. Agua Prieta
60. Gleeson, Courtland and Pearce
61. Yavapai

62. Boulder Dam
63. All of them
64. Colorado River
65. Coolidge (Calvin Coolidge)
66. Colorado River
67. Mazatzal Mountains
68. Flagstaff
69. Coconino
70. I-10
71. Phoenix
72. 392 miles at its maximum and 338 miles wide
73. Wickenburg
74. Prescott
75. Parker
76. La Paz
77. Mesa
78. Willcox Playa (Mormon Lake also acceptable as a wet one)
79. Apache
80. Colorado River
81. Douglas
82. Beeline Highway
83. The Coronado Trail
84. The Apache Trail
85. Santa Cruz or San Pedro
86. Santa Cruz
87. Springerville
88. Coronado
89. Saguaro, Canyon, Apache, and Roosevelt
90. Six: Laguna, Imperial, Parker, Davis, Hoover and Glen Canyon
91. Mount Agassiz (12,356 feet)
92. Coronado National Forest
93. Ponderosa
94. The Navajo
95. Roosevelt Lake (Theodore Roosevelt)
96. Gulf of California (Sea of Cortez)
97. Apache
98. Pinal Pioneer Parkway
99. Kofa (King of Arizona, or, K of A)
100. Mt. Wrightson (9,453 ft.)
101. Dragoon Mountains
102. Four Corners. Arizona, Utah, Colorado and New Mexico.
103. The Arizona Strip
104. Five: New Mexico, Colorado, Utah, Nevada, and California (Six, counting Sonora, Mexico)
105. U.S. Highway 66; *Route 66*
106. Cochise
107. Lake Powell
108. Central Avenue and Washington
109. Fort Mohave
110. Interstate 8
111. Mt. Lemmon, Santa Catalina Mountains
112. Monument Valley
113. Pah-Ute, lost to Nevada in 1866 (southeast corner of Nevada)
114. The Gila
115. Lake Havasu
116. Between Nogales and Yuma along the diagonal line of the Mexican border.
117. Santa Rita Mountains
118. Tonto National Monument
119. Pipe Springs National Monument
120. San Pedro

The Cacti of Arizona

"Arizona's cacti has more stickers than the bumper of a red-neck's pickup truck!"

In the weeks following the winter rains the desert literally springs to life as nature, in her inimitable creative genius, transposes the desert into a brilliant tapestry of panoramic beauty. Cactus blossoms and desert flowers burst forth with broad, bold brush strokes of colors upon the landscape. The sunscreen-like palo verde trees explode with a profusion of gold and the ironwood tree complements its grey-green leaves with a crown of beautiful pale violet blossoms. The flaming red torches atop the Ocotillo and the yucca with its magnificent white candelabra dispel the myth held by many that the desert is an uncompromising, barren, and forbidding place. They'll bloom only briefly, for the long, hot summer is not far behind and the hardy desert flora will have to consolidate their resources or "tighten up their belts" for the long, dry spell.

Basically, there are two principal groups of cacti, *cereus* and *opuntia*.

The *opuntia* is a jointed plant, its sections are linked to form a chain. Examples are the sausage-like links of the **Cholla** or the joined sections of the **Prickly Pear.** *Cereus* aren't united by plates or cylinders. Examples of these are the **Saguaro, Barrel** and **Organ Pipe** cacti.

The plant that most often comes to mind when one visualizes Arizona is the saguaro. This stately lord of the desert is one of the largest of the cactus family and grows almost exclusively in Arizona and Sonora, Mexico.

Native Americans have harvested its reddish fig-like fruit since prehistoric times. The juice can be fermented and is used traditionally by the Tohono O'odham Indians, who celebrate their New Year at the harvest in the summer months. In addition to eating the fruit, they historically used the ribs of the skeleton of this plant for building homes, traps and storage containers. The saguaro provides a safe refuge for many birds. Woodpeckers drill holes, open up small chambers, raise a family and then abandon their condos when the youngsters are ready to fly the coop. Elf owls, cactus wrens or other small birds then take up residence.

The saguaro is slow to grow. At the age of 9 years it stands only about 6 inches high. Around twenty, it undergoes an adolescent surge and grows maybe 2 inches a year. Sometime between age 30 to 50, saguaros will begin blooming. By the time they reach 80, saguaros may be 8 feet high. By age 150 they will grow to 35 to 50 feet in height. Saguaros can weigh between 15 and 20 tons (of which 98% is water), sprout a dozen or so arms, and live to a ripe old age of two hundred!

During times of good rainfall, the saguaro will expand its girth, accordion-like to absorb moisture to see it through the inevitable dry spells. A 4,000 pound saguaro will hold as much as 250 gallons of water. Too much rainfall can cause the arms to crack and cause serious damage. A prolonged freeze, say for more than 24 hours, can kill it.

Legend has it the barrel cactus is a good source of water in the desert. You can try it but you won't like it. The pulp can be crushed to create a liquid but the juice would peel the hide off the back of a Gila Monster. There are several species of the barrel cactus. The *Ferocactus* includes the Arizona, California and Sonora barrels. The *Echinocactus* includes the Many-headed, Mojave Pineapple and Blue barrels. Flowers grow briefly in the spring from the top of the stem near the growing point. The barrel only averages 5 to 6 feet in height at maturity. They are sometimes referred to as the "compass cactus" because they lean in a southwesterly direction.

In southern Arizona, near Ajo, another unique cactus, can be found. Named the Organ Pipe because of the way its arms branch out similar to the pipes of an organ, it is largely confined to this one general area. It also provides a fruit that has been harvested by Native Americans.

Prickly-pear cacti are found throughout the world. They are from the *Opuntia* group, the name coming from the pear shape of the flat pads attached to the stem. The large spines and tiny, almost invisible splinters can be singed off by fire and the pads can be eaten, quenching hunger and thirst at the same time. These cacti produce a dark red fruit that can be consumed by humans.

The *Coryphantha* are better-known as **Pincushions.** As the name implies, they resemble little pincushions. This group includes the Giant, Golden, Biscuit and Foxtail pincushions.

The *Echinocereus* makes up the group commonly known as **Hedgehogs.** They are relatively short-stemmed, usually no more than twenty inches in height and grow in clusters. They include the Claret Cup, Leding's, Fendler's, Robust, Strawberry and Arizona Rainbow cactus.

Leding's Hedgehog

The most notorious of the cactus plants are the chollas (choy-ahs). There are several species of these including the Buckhorn, Cane, Staghorn, Teddy Bear and, of course, the notorious Jumping cholla. The barbed spines embed themselves deep in the skin and are difficult to extract. It's wise to carry a large comb when venturing into the desert. Cholla balls are most easily removed from people, dogs and horses with a comb.

Incidentally, thorns on a desert plant are nature's way of preventing it from being fed upon by the many animals looking for food and moisture. Many thorny plants in the desert such as the **Joshua Tree, Ocotillo, Agave** and **Yucca** aren't cactus at all. The above-mentioned are all members of the *Lily* family. The yucca is more closely related to the garlic plant than to a cactus. The Native Americans had many uses of the long pointed stems of the yucca plant, including making sandals, needle and thread (just peel the tip back along the leaf), and twine. A shampoo is made from the roots.

The Agaves (ah-ga-ves), which include the Mescal or Century plant, Amole, Sotol and Desert Agave, resemble the Yucca and the two are often confused. However, the agave rosette grows close to the ground and looks like the bud of a giant artichoke. Pulque, tequila, and mescal are fermented or distilled from the agave plant.

Contrary to popular belief, the **Century Plant** does not live to be a hundred but has a life span of ten to seventy-five years. It blooms only once in its lifetime and spends that lifetime preparing for the grand occasion. When the time comes, it sends up a stalk which

Century Plant

might grow as much as a foot in a day, reaching a height of 15 to 30 feet. After blooming briefly, its life's work done, the Century Plant usually shrivels up and dies.

Another member of the *Lily* family, growing mostly in the high desert above Wickenburg is the Joshua Tree, tallest member of the desert Yuccas. The Joshuas have a unique appearance, their living leaves appearing dagger-like on the ends of numerous twisting arms. The arms and body, covered with dead leaves give the tree the look of a huge, hairy, abominable desert creature.

Joshua Tree

The Ocotillo (ah-co-ti-yah) is sometimes referred to as the "Monkey's Tail," or "Devil's Coachwhip." Actually, Ocotillo is Spanish for "coachwhip". It is kin to neither the cacti nor the *Lily* family, but related to the even stranger-looking Mexican Boojum tree. Most of the year the ocotillo appears to be dead, its sharp, grey thorns punctuating its long, thin limbs. But following a rain it comes to life, sprouting thousands of tiny, green leaves. As the weather dries once again, the leaves evolve into sharp thorns, protecting the plant from hungry animals. In the spring the ocotillo adorns its limbs with a beautiful orange-red torch-like blossom. Today, as in the past, Southwestern gardeners use ocotillo limbs woven into mesh wire to keep out pesky rabbits. Many of the limbs will take root, creating a living fence.

* * *

Sometimes the desiccating desert heat can be too much even for our hardy cacti. On June 26, 1990, the temperature hit 122 degrees in the Phoenix area. Several people in Cave Creek claimed they saw a saguaro pull itself out by the roots, walk over and hunker down 'neath the shade of a mesquite tree. A fisherman at Canyon Lake reported seeing a jumping cholla cactus leap into the lake to cool off. In Apache Junction a barrel cactus sneaked into town and tried to pass itself off as a fire hydrant.

There are a number of outlying communities in our state and, when it comes to discussing the weather, that's what some of them do best!

Cactus & Wildlife Trivia

1. What bird ranching industry was established in Phoenix and Yuma in the late 1800s?
2. Name the largest type of cactus in the world that is found in Arizona.
3. Name the official state reptile.
4. What dove is "sorrowful"?
5. What deadly spider is characterized by a violin-shaped spot on the upper side of it's head?
6. Name the state flower of Arizona.
7. What light-colored tree resembling a birch and nicknamed "quaking _____" is found in Arizona?
8. Why does a typical cactus have fluted (accordion-like) surfaces?
9. What wild pig-like critter resembling a small razorback is found in Arizona?
10. What cactus resembles "Mickey Mouse" ears?
11. What group of cacti does the "jumping cactus" belong to?
12. Name Arizona's largest game bird.
13. How can one best judge the age of a Saguaro cactus?
14. What is the common name for *Cereus giganteus*?
15. Which of the 30 species and subspecies of rattlesnakes is the most dangerous?
16. What are Abert, Kaibab, and Red?
17. What are Yucca, Agave and Ocotillo?
18. What is Arizona's state bird?
19. What desert plant has long arms and a scarlet-orange blossom and is sometimes referred to as a "Monkey's Tail"?
20. What cactus is also known as "Pitahaya"?
21. What is Arizona's colorful but deadly snake?
22. What red shape appears on female black widow spiders?
23. What small, slender Arizona animal has a tail that sticks straight up and a name that ends with the letter "i"?
24. Name the town in the Verde Valley that is named after a tree.

25. What "monster" is found in Arizona?
26. In Arizona, when speaking of "pronghorn" to what is one referring?
27. What is the wapiti more commonly called?
28. What popular bird can fly backwards and straight up?
29. What is Arizona's only native game fish?
30. What is the only poisonous lizard in the United States?
31. What is the plural of cactus?
32. What desert plant blooms only once in its lifetime?
33. What poisonous snake is characterized by "horns" above its eyes?
34. What is the name of the desert that includes both Phoenix and Tucson?
35. What snake is called the farmer's friend?
36. What is the largest game animal in Arizona?
37. What desert animal's name translates from Latin as "barking dog" (canis latrans)?
38. What animal hauled freight and mail in Arizona on an experimental basis during the 1850s?
39. Is an animal considered flora or fauna?
40. What cactus is called the "compass cactus" and leans in a southwesterly direction?
41. What group of cacti does the Teddy Bear cactus belong to?
42. What Arizona animal was most sought after by fur trappers of the early 1800s?
43. What are Hedgehog, Pincushion and Organ Pipe?
44. Name the official state mammal.
45. What is another name for the greasewood plant?
46. What is the desert's largest spider?
47. What is Arizona's oldest tree dating back some 1400 years?

48. Name one of the two common hawks found in the Sonoran Desert.
49. What is the name of Arizona's quail that has the fancy topknot?

Cactus & Wildlife Trivia Answers

1. Ostrich (their feathers were in great demand)
2. Saguaro
3. Ridge-nosed rattlesnake
4. Mourning dove
5. Brown Recluse
6. Saguaro cactus blossom
7. Aspen
8. To expand to hold and then gradually release water
9. Javelina (Have-a-lee-na)
10. Prickly Pear
11. Cholla
12. Wild turkey
13. By its height
14. Saguaro cactus
15. The Mohave rattlesnake. Its venom also attacks the neuro-system much like the cobra snake.
16. Types of squirrels found in Arizona
17. Desert plants (not cacti)
18. Cactus Wren
19. Ocotillo
20. Organ Pipe
21. Sonoran coral
22. An hourglass
23. Coatimundi
24. Cottonwood
25. Gila monster
26. Antelope
27. Elk
28. Hummingbird
29. Arizona trout
30. Gila monster
31. Cacti
32. Agave or Century plant. (Blooms once in 10 to 75 years.)
33. The sidewinder rattlesnake
34. Sonoran Desert
35. Gopher snake
36. Elk
37. Coyote
38. The camel
39. Fauna
40. Barrel
41. Cholla
42. Beaver
43. Cacti
44. Ringtail Cat
45. Creosote bush
46. Tarantula
47. Bristlecone pine
48. Harris or Red-Tail
49. Gambel's Quail

Engelmann's Prickly Pear

Arizona Weather Facts

"But it's a dry heat . . . . !"

Weather forecasters have it pretty easy in Arizona once they learn to correctly pronounce words like Ajo (ah-ho), Gila (hee-lah), Saguaro (sa-war-oh), Tsegi (sig-ee) Canyon, the Mazatzal (mah-sat-sail—pronounced locally mat-a-zell) Mountains and the Mogollon (muggy-ohn) Rim. Eighty-five per cent of the time the sun shines, so by predicting sunny weather every day, they'll be right 85% of the time. Forecasting the weather during Arizona's two rainy seasons—December, January and February, and the "monsoon" of July, August and early September—is more difficult. Still, it doesn't rain all that much during the rainy season, as some of the following records reveal. No two years are exactly alike. In January and February of 1993, Phoenix had more rain than Seattle, Washington. Then, the rains suddenly quit. It rained once in March but didn't rain again until August. That July, for the first time in recorded history (since 1895) no measurable rain fell. After a relatively dry rainy season, the clouds finally opened up in October, usually a dry month, and dropped record rains on the Phoenix area. It was so wet you could get 1% milk straight from the cow. It started out to be a wet winter but didn't end up that way. The winter of 1993-94 was one of the driest on record, and the cows went back to giving powdered milk. Experts blamed this strange phenomenon on the warming of the ocean's currents or *El Niño*. But, natives say that's how it's *always* been in the desert—a conundrum. Natives never lose faith. They have faith in that old cowboy axiom—"It always rains after a dry spell."

The most reliable weather indicator I've ever seen was up on the Colorado Plateau a few years ago. It was a weather rock and it was more accurate than the local forecaster with his fancy electronic weather-gathering data. This is how it works:

- ❖ A dry rock means fair weather.
- ❖ A wet rock means it's raining.
- ❖ A dusty rock means a dust storm.
- ❖ A swaying rock means the wind is blowing.
- ❖ A shadow under the rock means the sun is shining.
- ❖ A white rock means it's snowing.
- ❖ And, if its jumping up and down, an earthquake is upon us.

Most beautiful of all, the rock is not attached to its existence and doesn't mind which of the above is occurring.

* * *

Yes, the sun shines in southern Arizona—85% of the time and that's considerably more sunshine than Florida or Hawaii. Arizona also frequently has the nation's hottest and coldest temperatures on the same day. The **mean temperature** is 75 degrees average in the desert to 45 degrees in the high country. It usually gets meaner in the summer.

Record Heat: On June 28,1994, the temperature hit 128 degrees at Lake Havasu City.

Phoenix Heat Records: The highest in Phoenix was 122 degrees on June 26,1990. Phoenix has an average of 8 days of 110 degrees and above temperatures. The most 110+ days in Phoenix was 23 in 1983. The average day for the first 100-degree day is May 15 and the last is September 26. The record early 100-degree day was March 26,1988, and the record late was October 20, 1921 and 1949. By October most Arizonans are ready for a break in the heat but in 1991, October recorded 15 days of 100+ degrees. In 1993, the "monsoons" failed and Phoenix went 76 consecutive days over 100 degrees (another record.)

Record Rainfall: In 1978, Hawley Lake had 58.92 inches.

The **average rainfall** ranges from less than 3 inches per year in the southwest deserts to more than 30 inches per year in the White Mountains. Phoenix, at 1000 ft. elevation, averages about 7 inches a year while Tucson, elevation 2100 ft, averages about 11 inches annually. Flagstaff, at 7,000 ft. averages about 20 inches of moisture in a year. Areas in the White Mountains receive more than 30 inches of moisture annually. The wettest year in Phoenix was 1905, when 19.73 inches was recorded.

Record Drought: The driest year in Phoenix was 1956, when it rained only 2.82 inches. That same year it only rained .07 at Davis Dam on the Colorado River. The longest period without measurable rain (0.01 inch) in Phoenix history was 160 days, from December 30, 1971 to June 6, 1972. The longest period in Phoenix without even a trace of rain was 91 days, January 6 through April 5, 1984.

Record Snow: Hawley Lake also had the most snow in a single storm, 91 inches, on December 21, 1967. Arizona's snowiest winter was at Sunrise Mountain when it snowed 400.9 inches during the winter of 1972-73. Flagstaff averages 55 inches of snow annually while Prescott averages 25 inches.

Record Cold: The coldest day in Arizona was -40 degrees on January 7, 1971. The record cold for Phoenix was 16 degrees on January 7, 1913.

* Records are courtesy of *Ed Phillips' Arizona Almanac.*

Questionable Facts about the Weather and Climate of Arizona

Lukie and Melba Spurlock have been living in Payson for the past 68 years of their marriage. They both claim Payson has the healthiest climate in the whole USA. Even more remarkable, Lukie has never been to a doctor in that entire time. Early on, they agreed that when they got into an argument she'd go into the kitchen and he'd go outside and sit on the porch. He attributes his good health to all those years spent outdoors.

* * *

Arizona boasts some of the most notorious dust storms ever recorded. On July 19, 1973, Ira Gerlach was driving to his mobile home in Apache Junction when a huge dust storm hit. The dust was so thick he couldn't see ten feet ahead. Then, he spotted two taillights and decided to follow. This went on for several miles until suddenly he ran into the back end of a car. Ira jumped out and shouted at the driver, "Why didn't you signal before you stopped?"

"Why should I?" the other guy retorted, "I'm in my garage!"

* * *

On August 3, 1983, a single cloud passed over Why, Arizona and it began to rain. A tourist from nearby Ajo happened to be in town and he was so thrilled to see rain he got out of his car and stood in the middle of the town's main street and looked skyward, savoring the moment. Then, he looked around and saw the entire population of Why sitting on the porch of the general store giving him a hard stare. He felt like a sheepherder that'd just crashed a cattlemen's convention.

"Is something wrong?" he asked.

"Mister," one of them said, "We wish you'd get up here on the porch with the rest of us. It ain't rained around here in six months and we want all of it to hit the ground."

Senator Barry Goldwater was sitting out on the patio of his hilltop desert home the other day when a young man who'd recently moved to Arizona and was aspiring to run for political office came by to pay his respects.

The young man waited politely for the elder statesman to get in a conversational mood. Finally, Goldwater looked up at a scrawny cloud rolling in from the west. "I wonder if that's a serious cloud?" he wondered.

Wanting to make a good impression, the young man corrected, "Senator, I think you mean 'is that a cirrus cloud.' Actually I believe it's a cumulus cloud."

"Sonny," he growled, "Out here there's only two kinds of clouds—them that are serious and them that are not serious."

Weather Trivia

1. What was the hottest temperature ever recorded in Arizona?
2. Name the hottest town on record in Arizona.
3. What is the average annual rainfall in Phoenix, rounded to the nearest inch?
4. Why will people living in the Valley of the Sun never forget June 26, 1990?
5. What is the highest temperature ever recorded in Tucson?
6. What place holds the record for the coldest temperature ever recorded in Arizona?
7. What was significant about March 26, 1988?
8. Name the well-known Phoenix meteorologist and former state senator who publishes an annual weather almanac.

Weather Trivia Answers

1. Lake Havasu City, 128° F. on June 28, 1994.
2. Mohawk (1 in 3 days has averaged over 100°F over the past 100 years)
3. Seven inches
4. The temperature reached a record high of 122°F.
5. 117° F
6. Hawley Lake (-40°F, in 1971)
7. It was the earliest 100 degree day recorded in Phoenix.
8. Ed Phillips

Places to Go & Things to Do

Ski North America's southernmost ski slopes, visit "The Town Too Tough to Die", golf in Phoenix or tour the White Mountains—Arizona has it all!

Arizona has something for everybody. If you're an active outdoor sports enthusiast, there's both water and snow skiing, hiking, boating, biking, horseback riding and mountain climbing in all kinds of terrain. History buffs can poke around classic old towns like Tombstone, Bisbee, Globe, Flagstaff, Yuma and Prescott, or explore not-so-well-known ghostly villages like Paradise, Copperapolis, Harshaw or Bundyville. People come from all over the world to see the wideranging array of unique, near-pristine archaeological ruins, left behind by peoples who left, for reasons that remain a puzzle to this day. Each one has its own story to tell. Native Americans such as the Hopi and Navajo reside in remote parts of the state, many still living much the same as their ancestors have for centuries. Amateur geologists can examine rock formations that date back to the beginning of time. Plant lovers can study biotic life that runs the gamut of Merriam's Life Zones. Photographers can go on a "shutterbug safari" and find a myriad of beautiful scenery that challenges the creative camera eye.

If you prefer to sit back and let someone else do the driving, there are jeep and bus tours that will take you just about anywhere—and tell you all about it at the same time.

Arizona also offers a wide variety of spectator sports including professional rodeo, basketball, football, baseball, tennis, hockey and golf. Intercollegiate athletics at the major college level doesn't get any better than at the University of Arizona and Arizona State University.

For those who want to take a nostalgic journey back to those thrilling days of yesteryear, you can walk the streets with gunfighters on the prod at movie-set locations like Old Tucson or at Old West reproductions like Rawhide. Or, step back in history and stand on the spot where the real gunfighters faced off at Tombstone.

But you can't do Arizona in a day, or a week. Maybe not even in a lifetime. So you need to pace yourself. And it helps to do a little homework in advance. Before you go, read up on the places you intend to visit. Call the local chamber of commerce to ask specific questions. For accurate, up to date information on the little out-of-the-way places you might want to visit the Arizona section of your favorite bookstore.

The Arizona Department of Tourism, along with *Arizona Highways* magazine has divided the state into seven regions. I call 'em, *"The Magnificent Seven"*. There's more ways to regionalize this state than there are fleas on a hound dog's back. You may have your own ideas but this is a good way to start.

The **Canyon Country,** includes the Grand Canyon, Kaibab Plateau, Vermillion Cliffs, Marble Canyon, Flagstaff, Williams, the Grand Canyon Railway, Oak Creek, Sedona, Wupatki and Walnut Canyon.

Indian Country, includes Canyon de Chelly, Navajo and Hopi Reservations, Monument Valley, Navajo National Monument, Lake Powell, the Petrified Forest and Painted Desert.

The **Central Territory,** includes Prescott, the Verde Valley, the little railroad to Perkinsville, Jerome, the Bradshaw Mountains and Wickenburg.

The **High Country,** includes the White Mountains, Mogollon Rim, Pleasant Valley, Alpine, the Blue River country, Coronado Trail, and the Apache Reservations.

The **River Country**, includes a string of lakes and rivers, London Bridge, Yuma, the new gambling mecca across the river from Bullhead City at Laughlin, the ghost town of Oatman, and the entire western border of the state.

The **Golden Corridor,** includes Tucson and the greater Phoenix area where more than 80% of the state's population resides. Also included is the Pinal Parkway between Florence and Tucson, Picacho Peak, Superstition Mountains, Casa Grande National Monument, Arizona-Sonora Desert Museum, San Xavier del Bac Mission and the beautiful Saguaro National Monument.

The **Old West Country,** includes historic Tubac, Tumacacori National Monument, Tombstone and Bisbee. Also included is Organ Pipe National Monument, numerous ghost towns and lofty mountains.

Welcome to ARIZONA!

All are tourist-friendly and have comfortable accommodations that will suit everyone from the no-frills motels and hotels; to charming bed and breakfasts; to plush resorts.

Another way to organize your Arizona tour is to use either Tucson, Phoenix or Flagstaff as a base. For the past twenty years or so, I've led groups of college students and tourists on the following time-honored and road-tested *paseos* many times. Keep in mind, my itinerary is generalized and there's a whole lot more to see and do than I've listed. Keep an open mind for side trips; they can easily become the highlight of your *journada*.

Do plan ahead, and gather more detailed information on the specific places you plan to visit.

Things to do in Tucson

Tucson offers a variety of interesting and colorful places to visit including the Arizona-Sonora Desert Museum, Old Tucson, Saguaro National Monument, the Arizona Historical Society Museum, the Arizona State Museum on the University of Arizona campus, San Xavier del Bac Mission, the Pima Air Museum, Sabino Canyon and Mount Lemmon.

Beautiful **Sabino Canyon,** a riparian paradise, lures hikers, sightseers, photographers and creek-waders. **Mount Lemmon,** rising in the Santa Catalina Mountains at more than 9000 feet, offers great skiing in the winter and a cool escape from the desert heat in the summer. The 30-mile drive from Tucson up to Mount Lemmon takes only about an hour, yet you will travel through enough of Merriam's Life Zones to equate to a 2000-mile drive to Canada. At one o'clock in the afternoon you could be sweltering in the desert heat. An hour later you could be shivering among the Douglas firs and quaking aspens at 8,200 feet. And, it doesn't have to end there. A sky ride can take you up another 900 feet. **Ski Valley,** with 15 slopes, is the southernmost ski area in the United States. Mount Lemmon, incidentally, is named for Sara Plummer Lemmon, who climbed it back in 1881 while on her honeymoon.

A few miles east of Tucson is **Colossal Cave**, said to be the world's largest dry cavern. Parts of it are still unexplored. The cave served as a hiding place for train robbers and a legend of a lost treasure buried somewhere inside persists.

Downtown Tucson has a rich historical past that includes the Samaniego House, built in 1879; and the La Casa de Gobernador, a museum that was once the residence of Territorial Governor John C. Fremont and before that it was the home of the Leopaldo Carillo family.

The *La Fiesta de los Vaqueros* rodeo each February claims the world's longest non-mechanized parade. Tucson also has such cultural events as the Arizona Theater Company, Arizona Opera Company, the Tucson Symphony and Ballet Arizona.

Tucson has some of the state's finest resorts including the famous Arizona Inn, an Arizona landmark; Lowe's Ventana Canyon, at the foot of the beautiful Santa Catalina Mountains; The Westin La Paloma; the Sheraton El Conquistador; and the Tanque Verde Guest Ranch.

One of my favorite trips swings a wide loop from Tucson, goes down into Santa Cruz County, across Cochise County and joins Interstate 10 at Willcox. Going south from Tucson, be sure to visit the **Mission San Xavier del Bac,** the most beautiful mission in all the Southwest. Next stop at **Tubac,** the earliest Spanish settlement in Arizona, dating back to 1752. Nearby is the **Tumacacori** National Historical Park which contains the Tumacacori mission dating back to the days of Father Eusebio Kino, the legendary Jesuit "Padre on Horseback." Next stop is **Nogales.** Make sure to visit the **Pimeria Alta Historical Museum** on your way to a shopping spree south of the border.

Leaving Nogales, head east on State Route 82 along picturesque Sonoita Creek to Patagonia. Be sure to visit the **Patagonia-Sonoita Creek Sanctuary Wildlife Preserve.** South of town are the ghost towns of Mowry, Harshaw, Washington Camp and Duquesne. Don't forget to visit the Arizona wine country at **Elgin.** This picturesque country of hilly grasslands studded with clusters of oak trees has been the setting for such films as *"Oklahoma," "Monte Walsh,"* and *"Tom Horn."*

Your *journada* will take you by the majestic Huachuca Mountains and historic old **Fort Huachuca.** The Arizona Nature Conservancy has a sanctuary for some 15 species of hummingbirds in **Ramsey Canyon.** These mountains are also the home of Arizona State Balladeer **Dolan Ellis' Folklore Preserve.** The highway will eventually take you to **Tombstone**, the "Town Too Tough To Die." Here, legendary characters like John Slaughter, Wyatt Earp, Doc Holliday and Nellie Cashman walked the dusty streets. Plan to stay late—after those ubiquitous curio shops close. That's when the ghosts of old Tombstone come back to claim the streets.

A few miles down the road is **Bisbee,** the "Queen of the Copper Camps." Walking down streets with names like Tombstone Canyon and Brewery Gulch while gazing at the picturesque Victorian architecture takes you back to another time and place. Don't miss the tour down into the old **Copper Queen Mine.** Ride into the mine on ore cars driven by former miners and hear firsthand the stories of what working in the mines was really like. Plan to spend an evening sitting on the veranda of the historic **Copper Queen Hotel,** which has accommodated the likes of General John J. "Black Jack" Pershing and John Wayne. Next door is the **Mining and Historical Museum** which provides a thorough history of one of the West's greatest "copper camps."

From Bisbee, head east to **Douglas** and plan to at least have dinner at the historic **Gadsden Hotel,** the "last of the grand hotels." The Gadsden, with its marble columns, gold leaf ceiling and Tiffany stained-glass windows surrounding its spacious lobby is worth the entire trip to Douglas. The lobby served as a San Antonio opera house for the movie *"Life and Times of Judge Roy Bean,"* and a fancy Chicago hotel in *"Cowboy"*—a 1950s movie that starred Glenn Ford and Jack Lemmon.

A few miles east of Douglas, a museum stands on the grounds of "Texas John" Slaughter's old San Bernardino Ranch. Slaughter was also sheriff of Cochise County during the late 1880s and ended the career of many a rustler who "had too many irons in the fire."

From Douglas, head north towards the majestic **Chiricahua Mountains**—one of the best-kept secrets in Arizona. West of the mountains is the sprawling Sulphur Springs Valley—known to locals as the "Sufferin' Springs Valley." Plan to visit the Chiricahua National Monument and the **Wonderland of Rocks.** There are many roads leading into the mountains that will take you to green meadows and cool streams. Fishing is good on Rucker Lake and the road up Turkey Creek will take you past the grave of gunfighter Johnny Ringo. **Portal,** on the east slope of the mountains, is another birdwatchers paradise. The Chiricahuas gave songwriter Stan Jones the inspiration to write his classic song, *"Ghost Riders in the Sky."*

On the north end of the "cherry cows" are the skeletal ruins of historic old **Fort Bowie** and treacherous **Apache Pass** on the fabled **Butterfield Overland Stagecoach Line.** Stop to view the **Chiricahua National Monument.** From Fort Bowie, backtrack through the town of Dos Cabezas and rejoin Interstate 10 at Willcox.

I've made this loop in as little as two days— but that was pushing it—and taken as long as seven. Either way, you'll never see it all but it sure is fun trying.

Things to do in Phoenix

Because of its central location, Phoenix is the most convenient of the three largest Arizona cities. When visitors ask, "I'm only in Phoenix for the day. What should I do for a cultural experience?" I say,

"If you only have time to do one thing, do the **Heard Museum**." The Heard has one of the Southwest's best collections of Native American culture and art.

Nearby is the **Phoenix Art Museum**. A short drive down West Washington Street in downtown Phoenix will take you to the **Arizona Hall of Fame Museum** and the museum at the State Capitol. Out on East Washington is **Pueblo Grande Museum**. On the site are the excavations of a 13th century Hohokam village.

Pioneer Arizona Living History Museum is the state's rendition of Williamsburg, Virginia. This living museum, on I-17, a few miles north of Phoenix, offers a close-up look at the early days. The museum has a collection of 25 original and constructed buildings gathered from around the state that date from the 1860s to 1912. Costumed guides recreate life in a typical frontier community. Buildings include a bank, a Victorian home, opera house, blacksmith shop, miner's camp and more. Many of the buildings were removed from their original settings, located to the 550-acre site and restored.

For those who like hands-on experiences, there's horseback riding, jeep tours, bicycling, golf, tennis, boating, water-skiing, fishing, ice skating, surfing, camping and hiking. **Phoenix South Mountain Park** is the biggest municipal park in the world, containing almost 15,000 acres, mostly rugged wilderness. **Papago Park** offers picnicking, hiking, an 11-mile bike trail, the **Desert Botanical Garden**, horseback riding, the spring training home of the Oakland Athletics, an 18-hole golf course and the **Phoenix Zoo** with its Children's Trail.

Just east of Phoenix is **Tempe,** home of **Arizona State University** and the **Fiesta Bowl.** The town was named by an Englishman named Darrell Duppa, who was one of the first settlers in the Salt River Valley. One day he gazed out on that desert, strewn with creosote and prickly pear cactus and wryly observed it reminded him of the beautiful Vale of Tempe in Greece. Today, Tempe more closely resembles what Duppa thought he saw back in the 1870s. Downtown **Mill Avenue** has been beautifully restored to resemble a nostalgic turn-of-the-century American city street.

For those who like professional sports, the fabulous **Phoenix Suns** play basketball at the **America West Arena** from October until (hopefully) the NBA Finals in June each year. Major league baseball teams conduct spring training camps all over the Valley in February and March. For rodeo buffs, **Scottsdale's Parada Del Sol** is in February and Phoenix's own **Rodeo of Rodeos** is in March. Tempe's **Sun Devil Stadium** is home to the **Arizona Cardinals** of the National Football League. Ice Hockey's **Phoenix Roadrunners** square off with their opponents at the **Veteran's Memorial Coli-seum.** In 1996 the National Hockey League **Winnipeg Jets** moved to Phoenix to play at the America West Arena and became the **Coyotes.** And beginning in 1998 the **Arizona Diamondbacks** will play major league baseball in the new **Bank One Stadium** located near the America West Arena. The **Rattlers** play Arena Football during the summer at the America West Arena. The **Phoenix Open** golf tournament is played in stylish Scottsdale in January and several major tennis tournaments are held during the season. The Valley is also home to professional soccer and roller hockey teams.

Phoenix West Loop

I prefer "loop trips" and here's a good one for those who like to travel the river country of western Arizona. Head southwest towards the historic river crossing at Yuma. Be sure to visit the **Yuma Territorial Prison,** source of many an Arizona tale. The **Century House Museum** provides a myriad of information on one of the state's most historical cities. The strategic river crossing at the confluence of the Gila and Colorado Rivers predates the arrival of men from Coronado's expedition in 1540. During the California Gold Rush the Yuma Crossing was an important stagecoach stop and river port for steamboats plowing their way up the Colorado.

From Yuma, follow the Colorado River northward to Martinez Lake and the **Imperial National Wildlife Refuge.** East of you on Highway 95 to Quartzsite is the **Kofa National Wildlife Refuge.** At **Lake Havasu City** a quaint English village surrounds the fabled **London Bridge.** During the 1960s the 130-year-old bridge was dismantled brick by brick and hauled to Arizona where it was reconstructed. Today it is one of the state's major tourist attractions. Further north is the **Havasu National Wildlife Refuge.** Try your luck at the riverside gambling mecca at **Laughlin, Nevada,** just across the river from Bullhead City. From there go north to the old gold mining town of **Oatman.** Old **Route 66** will take you over treacherous Oatman Pass, past the ghost town of Goldroad and into **Kingman.** If you don't choose to add **Lake Mead, Hoover Dam** and the **Lake Mead National Recreation Area** to your itinerary, get on State Route 93 and return to Phoenix by way of **Wickenburg.** If you like traveling the high desert country, this one's a sure winner.

Phoenix North Loop

Another great loop trip out of Phoenix is to head north on Interstate 17, stopping at **Montezuma's Castle National Monument.** Here prehistoric Sinagua Indians built mud dwellings in the alcoves of the cliffs above Beaver Creek around A.D. 1200. Take the exit off the interstate on State Route 179 leading into **Sedona** and **Oak Creek Canyon.** For those who don't have much time and want to see as much of the state's diversity, this is one I always recommend. It offers spectacular scenery, prehistoric ruins like **Tuzigoot,** a frontier military post at **Camp Verde,** wilderness areas such as **Sycamore Canyon,** a scenic railroad called the **Verde River Canyon Railroad,** and a boom town-turned-ghost town-turned-art colony at **Jerome**. Perched precariously on the steep slopes of Cleopatra Hill, Jerome was one of the richest rip-snortin' copper camps in the West during its heyday. Due to the discovery of rich ore beneath the town, miners used hundreds of thousands of tons of dynamite to blast. Naturally, this caused the town to slide down Cleopatra Hill. During the 1930s, Jerome was said to be a city "on the move." Unfortunately, like the stock market, it was all downhill.

State Route 179 will take you back to the interstate, but if time permits, drive on over **Mingus Mountain** to Arizona's first territorial capital at **Prescott.** Prescott is a one-of-a-kind Arizona city.

Prescott was founded as the territorial capital in 1864. Prospectors' picks and shovels had turned up rich deposits of gold in the area and a tiny settlement of crude log cabins sprang up nearby. Prescott is nestled among pine forests, mountains, lakes and meadows and its mile-high climate is ideal year around. It is continually selected as one of the most desired locations to live in the entire United States.

Don't forget to visit the **Sharlot Hall Museum.** On the grounds are some classic Victorian homes of early residents, along with the log territorial capital building. In the heart of Prescott is the historic old county courthouse, the Rough Rider statue and a shady plaza. Beautiful Victorian-style homes, some converted into bed and breakfast inns, are located along Union Street, near the plaza. North of town, is the **Phippen Museum of Western Art,** named for George Phippen, one of the founders of the Cowboy Artists of America. Prescott's **Frontier Days** is an annual July Fourth community celebration with the world's oldest professional rodeo and parade. Don't miss seeing

notorious **"Whiskey Row,"** where cowboys used to come to "oil up their insides," on a Saturday night. One hot July evening in 1900 the town caught fire. The fancy backbar at the old Palace Bar was in danger of going up in smoke and would have, had it not been for the alert patrons who hoisted it, along with all the booze, and carried the whole works across the street to safety. They also saved the piano. That night, while Prescott burned, the backbar was opened for business and the piano player resumed his playing. The most requested tune that night was, *"There'll Be A Hot Time In The Old Town Tonight."*

Now you have more options. You can follow State Route 69 back through the communities of **Dewey, Humboldt** and **Mayer** to the interstate. Or, you can take the scenic route south out of Prescott on U.S. 89 through the mountains on the **White Spar Highway,** down past **Peeples Valley, Kirkland, Yarnell** (plenty of side trips like over to **Skull Valley,** along the way,) and on down to **Wickenburg** and back to Phoenix.

Plan to stay awhile "Out Wickenburg Way." Downtown Wickenburg has a wonderful western flavor with its frontier architecture. It is known as the **"Dude Ranch Capital of the World."** Many of these are real working ranches where greenhorns are given a chance to "cowboy up." Don't miss the **Desert Caballeros Western Museum.**

Wickenburg was named for an old prospector named Henry Wickenburg who found a rich lode of gold back in 1863. The legendary **Vulture Mine** was the most famous gold mine in Arizona history. Downtown is the notorious Jail Tree. Locals were so busy digging for gold they didn't have time to build a jail so they just chained the bad guys and gals up to a tree. The Hassayampa River runs through Wickenburg. Tongue-in-cheek locals erected a sign saying "No Fishing" on the bridge. That river has water in it so seldom that the fish have all forgotten how to swim.

For another northbound loop, take I-17 north to **Camp Verde** and go east on State Route 260. This trip is mostly scenic forest and will take you into the high country above the **Mogollon Rim** and back down again past **Strawberry** and **Pine.** Both Strawberry and Pine have a small town friendliness that reminds one of bygone days in Arizona.

Just south of Pine is the **Tonto Natural Bridge,** the world's largest travertine bridge. You can easily fit an 11-story building beneath its arch. It's a great place to have a picnic, or spend the day.

Payson, nestled in the pines in the heart of the Mogollon Rim country, boasts the healthiest climate in America.

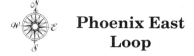

Phoenix East Loop

Another good loop trip out of Phoenix heads east towards **Apache Junction.** Apache Junction offers several options, depending on your mood. If you want lakes, head up the **Apache Trail** to the old tumbledown mining town of **Goldfield.** A vista beyond Goldfield provides a spectacular view of the fabled **Superstition Wilderness.** Somewhere out there in that rugged wilderness lies the treasure of Jacob Waltz in the legendary **"Lost Dutchman Mine".** The real treasure lies in the beauty of the place. Don't forget to visit the **Lost Dutchman Museum.**

The road leads past **Canyon Lake** stopping at **Tortilla Flat,** a good place to dine and enjoy the Old West ambiance. Just past Tortilla Flat, the pavement ends. The dirt road twists and winds down **Fish Creek Hill** and passes **Apache** and **Roosevelt** lakes. At Roosevelt, you can go left and head for **Punkin Center** and loop around back to Phoenix on State Route 87. Or, you can turn right and go into the former rip-roaring mining town of **Globe,** the hometown of many famous Arizonans, including former Governor Rose Mofford. From there, you can travel through **Miami,** on U.S. 60, down through some beautiful canyon country to **Superior** and back to Phoenix.

Another option out of Apache Junction is to go east on U.S. 60 to Superior, head southeast on State Route 177, past **Kearny, Hayden** and **Winkleman.** At the junction of the Gila and San Pedro Rivers, go south past Aravaipa Creek to **Mammoth.** From Mammoth go south on State Route 77 past **Oracle** to **Biosphere II.** At **Oracle Junction,** turn right on U.S. 89 and go northwest on the **Pinal Pioneer Parkway** on your way back to Phoenix. You'll see the beautiful Sonoran Desert in all its splendor. Be sure and stop off in **Florence** and visit the town's nostalgic main street on your way home.

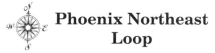

Phoenix Northeast
Loop

For another, longer trip out of Phoenix, take State Route 87 (the Beeline) north to **Payson,** then go east on State Route 260 to **Show Low,** the gateway to the beautiful **White Mountains.** From Show Low you can loop back to Phoenix on U.S. 60 down the Salt River Canyon to Globe and home. Or, you can drive east on 260 past **Pinetop** and on to **Springerville.** From Springerville go south on U.S. 191 to **Alpine** and follow the scenic **Coronado Trail** past Hannagan Meadow to **Clifton** and **Safford,** then back along U.S. 70 to Globe and home again. There is a magnificent lookout spot just above **Morenci** and **Clifton.** Just a note; this road is not for the faint of heart.

Things to do in Flagstaff

Historically, Flagstaff has been the hub of culture, commerce and transportation for northern Arizona. The place got its name back in 1876, after a party of colonists from Boston, who were camped there on July 4th, hung the flag on a skinny ponderosa pine in honor of the nation's centennial. They'd come to the area in hopes of starting a farming community in the lush meadows at the foot of the **San Francisco Mountains.** Flagstaff's short growing season (9 months winter, 3 months poor sledding) made the place seem more conducive to sightseeing, so they moved on.

Unlike her sisters to the south, Flagstaff has four distinct seasons with summer temperatures averaging a high of only 80 degrees and winter highs averaging a comfortable 43 degrees.

Flagstaff is at an altitude of 7,000 feet and surrounded by the 1.8 million-acre **Coconino National Forest,** a vast area of forests, meadows, lakes, canyons and the mystical San Francisco Mountains. Reaching heights of over 12,600 feet, these towering peaks are sacred places to both the Navajo and Hopi Indians.

The San Francisco range is also the home of the **Arizona Snow Bowl,** one of the state's most popular ski resorts. During the winter skiers can zip down any one of more than 30 slopes. The chairlift, which also operates in the summer, is a mile-plus "sky-ride" providing spectacular vistas of the high country.

There's always something going on in Flagstaff for visitors and locals alike. **Winterfest** takes place in February. The **"Trappings** of the American West" starts in May. The **Flagstaff Festival for the Arts** starts in June, as does the **Route 66 Festival**. The **Flagstaff Festival of the Pines** is in August. **Northern Arizona University,** the **Museum of Northern Arizona,** and the **Coconino Center for the Arts** are the cultural centers. Along with wonderful hiking trails in the wilderness, there is **Wupatki National Monument** and **Walnut Canyon National Monument,** ancient dwellings of the prehistoric Sinagua Indians. **Riordan State Park** honors one of the pioneer families in Flagstaff. And at **Lowell Observatory** where the planet Pluto was discovered back in the 1930s lecture tours and observations are held throughout the year.

(See the *Phoenix North Loop* information for loops into the area south of Flagstaff and the Sedona-Verde Valley.)

For a nostalgic trip to the **Grand Canyon,** take Interstate 40 west to **Williams** and climb aboard the **Grand Canyon Railway.** Or, if you prefer to drive, take U.S. 180 north out of Flagstaff, past the San Francisco Mountains and up to the Grand Canyon. Include a visit to the **I-MAX Theater** at **Tusayan.** Dining at historic **El Tovar** on the Canyon's rim is a memorable event. Neither words nor photographs have been able to sufficiently describe the Canyon. It's something you'll have to see for yourself and must be seen at different times of the day to capture the variable moods. Escape the crowd and take a stroll along the Canyon's edge and find a place to be alone with your thoughts—just you and the Canyon. The ambiance sets the tone for some introspective reflection.

Wupatki and the smaller *Wukoki* ruins in the Wupatki National Monument near Sunset Crater.

Photos Courtesy J. Wade, Jr.

Going east from the village at Grand Canyon, take State Route 64 to the historic trading post at **Cameron.** If you've run out of time, head south on U.S. 89 towards Flagstaff. Be sure to stop at **Wupatki National Monument** on the way. I consider these red-rock ruins, with the San Francisco Peaks as a backdrop, one of the most beautiful prehistoric cities in the Southwest.

If time permits, go north at Cameron up U. S. 89 to **Bitter Springs** and east across the bridge at **Marble Canyon.** A short side trip will take you to **Lee's Ferry,** an earlyday river crossing for Mormon pioneers moving to Arizona. River rafting expeditions through the Grand Canyon are launched from here.

Traveling west along the foot of the spectacular **Vermillion Cliffs,** you can watch the hues change with the time of day. A steep climb up onto the **Kaibab Plateau** will take you to **Jacob Lake.** Drive south 45 miles and you'll come to the fabulous **North Rim of the Grand Canyon,** a thousand feet higher in elevation than the South Rim.

A view from the North Rim of the Canyon.

(Photo courtesy J. Wade, Jr.)

You can extend your trip to include some of Utah's colorful country by heading north from Jacob Lake to **Fredonia,** then northwest to **Zion National Park.** From Zion head northeast to **Bryce Canyon,** then south again to Kanab, Utah. Follow U.S. 89 to **Lake Powell.** Be sure to take the riverboat trip to **Rainbow Bridge.** From **Page,** take U.S. 89 back home to Flagstaff.

A variation of the above trip would be to head north of **Cameron** then east on U.S. 160 into Navajo-Hopi country. At **Tuba City** you have two choices. You can go east on State Route 264 to the **Hopi Mesas** or, northeast to State Route 564 (just below Kayenta) and north to visit the **Navajo National Monument.** Don't miss your chance to climb down **Tsegi Canyon** to see the beautiful cliff dwelling, **Betatakin.** Returning to 264, go east to **Kayenta** and drive 19 miles north to magnificent **Monument Valley** and **Gouldings Trading Post.** The Valley boasts some of the world's most beautiful buttes, mesas and spires.

From Monument Valley it's about a three-hour trip back to Flagstaff by way of Kayenta, Tuba City and Cameron.

Places to Go & Leisure Trivia

1. What Arizona city's name means big house?
2. What should you *not* wear to the Pinnacle Peak Patio Restaurant?
3. What Tucson resort hotel's name means "the conqueror" in Spanish?
4. In what city is Fort Whipple Veterans Hospital located?
5. What is northeast Arizona's most famous trading post, now a National Historic Site?

The *Hi Jolly Monument* commemorates **Hadji Ali,** a citizen of Turkey who came to America to handle a fleet of camels from the Middle East intended to transport supplies across the Southwest from Texas to California during the 1850's.

(Photo courtesy J. Wade, Jr.)

6. Where is the monument to camel driver Hi Jolly (Hadji Ali) located?
7. Where is Phantom Ranch located?
8. What two cactus forests, both national monuments, are located in Pima County?
9. From what country did Tempe derive its name?
10. What anniversary did Tucson celebrate in 1975?
11. Where is Bell Rock?
12. Name the crater near Winslow that is almost one mile across.
13. Who is called the "The angel of the mining camps"?
14. Where might one find Fred Flintstone in Arizona?
15. Whose name is associated with lodging and restaurants at the Grand Canyon?
16. Name the well-known geological and cultural museum at Flagstaff.

17. What former southern Arizona boomtown's name was synonymous with pumpkins and gourds?

18. What is the Phoenix metropolitan area affectionately referred to as?

19. What desert community is jokingly called the "Fan Belt Capital of the World"?

20. What city has the Rosson House?

21. What city was the center of Arizona's sheep industry in the late 1800s?

22. Where is Buckey O'Neill Hill?

23. What city is sometimes referred to as the Concentrator City?

24. Where is Tlaquepaque? (T-lockay-pockay)?

25. What is located on the site of the historic Ingleside Resort golf course?

26. Name one Arizona community with the same name as a U.S. President.

27. Within 50 feet, how high is the world's highest fountain at Fountain Hills?

28. Name the Air Force base located in Maricopa County.

29. Name one of the two largest sundials in North America.

30. Name one of Arizona's "mile-high" cities.

31. What city is located in Tombstone Canyon?

32. Where is the world's largest rose tree?

33. What is the highest concrete dam in the United States?

34. What are Ruby, Gillette and Gunsight?

35. Name Arizona's third largest city.

36. What city is named after an Arizona governor whose name began with the letter "S"?

37. What was the original name of Colorado City?

38. What are Davis and Horse Mesa?

39. What city takes its name from a July 4th ceremony?

40. Where is Arizona's U.S. Marine Corps Air Station?

41. Name the world's largest retirement community.

42. At what site did the Earp brothers, Doc Holliday, the Clanton's and the McLaury's shoot it out?

43. What is another name for "Free Woman", Arizona?

44. What territorial governor has a commemorative home in both Prescott and Tucson?

45. Where are the White House Ruins?

46. In 1989, the town of Williams held a gala celebration for what?

47. In what Arizona community did Reverend Endicott Peabody establish his first church?

48. What is the county seat of Graham County?

49. What famous Hohokam Indian structure is near Coolidge?

50. What is the best known "well" in northern Arizona?

51. Name Arizona's only frontier military post still active today.

52. Where is the original Gadsden Hotel located?

53. Name one of the most well-known birding areas in southern Arizona.

54. Where are the Gold Rush Days?

55. Where is the Shrine of the Ages Chapel?

56. What southern Arizona city derives its name from the Indian Word *chukshon* meaning dark base?

57. What is Puerto Peñasco better known as?

58. What is the nearest community to Schnebly Hill?

59. What town received its name from a card game?

60. What city is home to "Whiskey Row"?

61. What community is located near Mt. Lemmon?

62. What city is referred to as the gateway to Hoover Dam and Las Vegas?

63. What is Scottsdale's nickname?

64. What large dam is located on the Gila River southeast of Globe?

65. Where is Slide Rock?

66. What is the complete name of Arizona's largest planetarium?

67. Where is the "Hummingbird Capital of the World"?

68. What ski area is in the Santa Catalina Mountains?

69. What lake is directly south of Roosevelt Dam?

70. Where is the picturesque Chapel of the Holy Cross?

71. What ancient Hopi village sits on a narrow rock tabletop?

72. What national park in Arizona has to partially close down during the winter?

73. With what Arizona site are the words "El Tovar" associated?

74. Where are Wyatt Earp Days held?

75. Where in Arizona was the westernmost battle of the Civil War fought?

76. What is the highest single steel arch bridge in the country?

77. Name the "Most Heavenly Trail" into the Grand Canyon.

78. What "happy-go-lucky" community was developed by Tom Darlington and K.T. Palmer?

79. What Arizona community is named for a cousin of Winston Churchill's mother?

80. What castle is located in Yavapai County?

81. Where is Eastern Arizona College located?

82. What Arizona city once had the names of Buena, Garden Canyon and Frye?

83. Name Arizona's pioneer luxury resort developed by Dr. A. J. Chandler.

84. What famous natural bridge is near Lake Powell?

85. Name the city that is home to Northern Arizona University (NAU).

86. What is the largest city park in the world and where is it located?

87. What is the name of Tucson's annual rodeo parade?

88. Name the community located near the entrance to Canyon de Chelly (pronounced canyon-de-shay).

89. What community was named for Ellsworth Schnebly's sister-in-law?

90. Name the national monument near Clarkdale that overlooks the Verde River.

91. Where is McFarland State Park?

92. Name the city located between Tucson and Phoenix that has the same name as a city in Italy.

93. What is Tumacacori?

94. What Arizona city has three county courthouses?

95. Name the national monument located near Roosevelt Lake.

96. What is known as the "White Dove of the Desert"?

97. What Arizona city is the Boyce Thompson Southwestern Arboretum near?

98. Where did Frank Lloyd Wright live and work (near Scottsdale)?

99. What is the world's deepest dam?

100. What is the name of the futuristic 20-story cliff dwelling being built near Cordes Junction?

101. What is the nation's largest man-made lake (by volume)?

102. What famous street is located in Bisbee?

103. What are Coffee Pot, Tea Pot, and Merry-go-round?

104. What Arizona landmark previously graced the Thames River?

105. Where is the Lavender Pit?

106. Where is the Copper Queen Hotel?

107. What is the common name of the road to Roosevelt Lake?

108. Name the popular gambling town on the Colorado River across from Bullhead City

109. What small, eastern Arizona community owns its own prehistoric ruins?

110 On which Indian Reservation is the Sunrise Ski Area located?

111. Who is entombed in a pyramid in Phoenix's Papago Park?

112. Name the town west of Phoenix that is named for a tire company.

113. Where is 800 ft. Spider Rock located?

114. What famous Sinagua Indian cliff dwelling is located in the Verde Valley?

115. Name the oldest continuously occupied town in America.

116. February 14 has an extra special meaning to which Arizona community?

117. Name the experimental project near Oracle, Arizona that is an independent, self-contained three-acre living habitat.

118. Name the central Arizona mining town that has the same name as a large city in Florida.

119. What northern Arizona community is named after a small red fruit?

120. What street, having the same name, is adjacent to both Arizona State University and the University of Arizona?

121. What town derives its name from the old Spanish pronunciation of the Biblical phrase, "My God, My God, why hast thou forsaken me?"

122. In what city is Penitentiary Avenue?

123. Name the world's largest travertine bridge.

124. What famous cave is southeast of Tucson?

125. What is the name of Tucson's desert museum?

126. What place was once known as the dude ranch capital of Arizona?

127. Where is Fred L. Whipple Observatory?

128. What area did Harry Goulding and Josef Muench make famous?

129. What city boasts of having the cleanest air in North America?

130. What town was founded in 1878 on a square mile tract of table land?

131. Name the native son and popular Tempe mayor for 16 years for whom the city's government complex is named?

132. Name the capital city of the Navajo Nation.

133. Where is Arizona Western College located?

134. What Scottsdale site is modeled after the Italian town of San Gimignano?

135. In what city is the American Graduate School of International Management?

136. What man-made symbol is on Tucson's Sentinel Peak?

137. What southern Arizona town's name means mountain view?

138. Where is Arizona's most famous truck stop? (Hint: it's also a Dolan Ellis song title.)

139. What is the name given to Prescott's famous street of saloons?

140. What well-known Grand Canyon resort hotel is also a National Historic Site?

141. For what Arizona city would Ohio natives have an affinity.

142. What is the other name of Tucson's "A Mountain"?

143. What town's main street is Deuce of Clubs?

144. What town was named for two men—one a Mormon apostle and the other a rancher?

145. What Arizona town's name means "garlic"?

146. Name the Phoenix park and museum that was once a prehistoric Hohokam village.

147. For what breed of horse is Scottsdale renowned?

148. Where in Arizona is one of the United States Army's two worldwide communication centers?

149. Where is Weaver's Needle?

150. What is Arizona's #1 tourist attraction?

151. The name of what Arizona city means walnuts?

152. Where is the world's largest collection of telescopes found?

153. What well-known "ghost town" is built on a hill?

154. Where are "Helldorado Days" held?

155. Name the village that has the nation's only post office where mail is received and sent out by mule.

156. Where is notorious Allen Street?

157. What is the hometown of singing cowboy Rex Allen?

158. Where is the World Championship Burro Biscuit Toss held?

159. What is the county seat of Navajo County?

160. Name Litchfield Park's Five-Star Resort.

161. What famous lost mine is in Z-shaped Sno-ta-hay Canyon?

162. What Arizona city is home to "London Bridge"?

163. Name the Arizona resort hotel founded by black cattleman and stage company owner Bill Neal.

164. Where is the world's largest solar telescope located?

165. What city is Lyman Recreational Area near?

166. What city is called the Gateway to the Rim?

167. Where is Yavapai Community College?

168. What city was established as a result of the building of Glen Canyon Dam?

169. What well-known Arizona city was almost named Utleyville?

170. What is the name of Arizona's living historical museum north of Phoenix?

171. What city has Santa Fe as its main avenue?

172. Where are "Andy Devine Days" held?

173. Name two of Arizona's four towns that have Christmas names.

174. What city is the Gateway to the Grand Canyon?

175. What is the smallest state park in Arizona?

176. Who is Gurley Street in Prescott named for?

177. Where is the Agate Bridge?

178. Where is an anchor from the USS Arizona on display in Arizona?

179. Where is the Bird Cage Theater?

180. What is the capital of Arizona's neighbor, Sonora, Mexico?

181. Name the mountain peak where the University of Arizona/Smithsonian multiple mirror telescope is located.

182. Where is Mars Hill?

183. Name the only active airport owned by the State of Arizona.

184. In 1864, Gimletville was a proposed name for what city?

185. Where was the nation's first municipal airport built?

186. What city is now located where the well-known Sunset

Crossing was in the 1800s?

187. Name the town best known for its easy living and Easy Street.

188. What city hosts the annual Parada del Sol?

189. The four clocks on the old Florence courthouse are set at what time?

190. Where is the oldest active livery stable in America?

191. What city is the Gateway to the Land of Cochise?

192. On what cone-shaped hill does Jerome perch?

193. What Gila Indian Reservation lake is located south of Phoenix?

194. Name the world's tallest masonry dam.

195. Name the city that has had 4 flags flown over it and name the 4 flags.

196. What Arizona city was named for a well-known American historian?

197. Where does the annual federally sanctioned (and oldest of its kind in America) Pony Express ride originate?

198. What Arizona man-made recreation pool holds 4,000,000 gallons of water?

199. What is Tucson's nickname?

200. What city hosts the Rodeo of Rodeos?

201. What Indian tribe lives on the San Xavier Reservation?

202. What are Surprise and Why?

203. What frontier military post was located near Tucson?

204. What trail was formerly known as the Cameron Trail?

205. What community calls itself "The Town too Tough to Die?"

206. Where are Frontier Days held?

Places to Go & Leisure
Trivia Answers

1. Casa Grande
2. A necktie
3. Tucson's El Conquistador (Sheraton)
4. Prescott
5. Hubbell Trading Post
6. Quartzsite
7. At the bottom of the Grand Canyon
8. Saguaro and Organ Pipe National Monuments
9. Greece (Vale of Tempe)
10. Bicentennial (200 years)
11. Sedona
12. Meteor Crater
13. Nellie Cashman
14. Bedrock City (Valle), on the road to the Grand Canyon
15. Fred Harvey
16. Museum of Northern Arizona
17. Calabasas
18. Valley of the Sun
19. Gila Bend
20. Phoenix
21. Flagstaff
22. Bisbee
23. Miami
24. Sedona
25. Arizona Country Club
26. Coolidge, Roosevelt, Johnson, Taylor and Fort Grant
27. 560 feet
28. Luke Air Force Base
29. Carefree and Sun City's sundials
30. Prescott or Bisbee
31. Bisbee
32. Rose Tree Inn, Tombstone
33. Hoover Dam
34. Arizona ghost towns
35. Mesa
36. Safford
37. Short Creek
38. Arizona Dams
39. Flagstaff
40. Yuma
41. Sun City
42. The O.K. Corral, Tombstone
43. Fredonia
44. John C. Fremont
45. Canyon de Chelly
46. Reopening of the Grand Canyon Railway
47. Tombstone (St. Paul's Episcopal)
48. Safford
49. Casa Grande National Monument
50. Montezuma Well
51. Fort Huachuca
52. Douglas
53. Madera, Portal and Ramsey Canyons
54. Wickenburg
55. Grand Canyon
56. Tucson
57. Rocky Point
58. Sedona
59. Show Low
60. Prescott
61. Summerhaven
62. Kingman
63. "The West's Most Western Town"
64. Coolidge Dam
65. Oak Creek Canyon (near Sedona)
66. Grace Flandrau Planetarium (University of Arizona, Tucson)

67. Ramsey Canyon
68. Mount Lemmon
69. Apache Lake
70. Sedona
71. Walpi
72. Grand Canyon National Park, North Rim
73. Grand Canyon (El Tovar is a hotel there)
74. Tombstone
75. Picacho Pass
76. Glen Canyon Bridge (U.S. 89)
77. Bright Angel Trail
78. Carefree
79. Jerome (Eugene Jerome)
80. Montezuma Castle National Monument
81. Thatcher
82. Sierra Vista
83. San Marcos Hotel (1912)
84. Rainbow Bridge
85. Flagstaff
86. South Mountain Park; Phoenix
87. La Fiesta de los Vaqueros
88. Chinle
89. Sedona (Sedona N. Schnebly)
90. Tuzigoot
91. Florence
92. Florence
93. Early Spanish mission south of Tucson and a National Monument
94. Florence
95. Tonto National Monument
96. San Xavier del Bac Mission
97. Superior
98. Taliesen West
99. Parker Dam (Lake Havasu)
100. Arcosanti
101. Lake Mead
102. Brewery Gulch
103. Rocks (or streets) in Sedona
104. London Bridge at Lake Havasu City
105. Bisbee
106. Bisbee
107. Apache Trail
108. Laughlin
109. Springerville (Casa Malpai)
110. Apache (Fort Apache Reservation)
111. Governor George Hunt and members of his family
112. Goodyear
113. Monument Canyon (Canyon de Chelly)
114. Montezuma Castle
115. Old Oraibi (Hopi Mesas)
116. Valentine
117. Biosphere II
118. Miami
119. Strawberry or Cherry
120. University
121. Eloy
122. Yuma
123. Tonto Natural Bridge near Pine
124. Colossal Cave
125. Arizona-Sonora Desert Museum
126. Wickenburg
127. Mount Hopkins (south of Tucson)
128. Monument Valley (promoted it to Hollywood)
129. Flagstaff (Payson is also acceptable)
130. Mesa
131. Harry Mitchell
132. Window Rock
133. Yuma
134. The Borgata
135. Glendale
136. The letter "A" for University of Arizona
137. Sierra Vista

138. Tuba City
139. Whiskey Row
140. El Tovar (opened in 1905)
141. Buckeye
142. Sentinel Peak
143. Show Low
144. Snowflake (Erastus Snow and William J. Flake)
145. Ajo
146. Pueblo Grande
147. Arabian horses
148. Fort Huachuca
149. Superstition Mountains
150. Grand Canyon
151. Nogales
152. Kitt Peak
153. Jerome
154. Tombstone
155. Supai, Grand Canyon
156. Tombstone
157. Willcox
158. Oatman
159. Holbrook
160. The Wigwam
161. Lost Adam's Mine
162. Lake Havasu City
163. Mtn. View Hotel (Oracle)
164. Kitt Peak
165. St. Johns
166. Payson
167. Prescott
168. Page
169. Scottsdale
170. Pioneer Arizona
171. Flagstaff
172. Kingman
173. Christmas, Santa Claus, Snowflake and Silver Bell
174. Williams
175. Tombstone Court House State Park
176. John Gurley, Arizona's first appointed territorial governor (He died before taking office.)
177. Petrified Forest National Monument (largest petrified log)
178. The State Capitol mall
179. Tombstone
180. Hermosillo
181. Mt. Hopkins, near Tucson.
182. Flagstaff
183. Grand Canyon Airport
184. Prescott
185. Tucson, 1919
186. Winslow
187. Carefree
188. Scottsdale
189. 9 o'clock
190. Grand Canyon (since 1902)
191. Benson
192. Cleopatra Hill
193. Firebird Lake
194. Roosevelt Dam
195. Tucson (Spain, Mexico, The United States of America and the Confederate flag)
196. Prescott (William Hickling Prescott)
197. Holbrook. Holbrook's Hashknife Gang carries the U.S. Mail to open Scottsdale's Parada del Sol.
198. Big Surf, Tempe
199. The Old Pueblo
200. Phoenix
201. Tohono O'odham (formerly called Papago)
202. Arizona communities
203. Fort Lowell
204. Bright Angel Trail (Grand Canyon)
205. Tombstone
206. Prescott

Travel Trivia

Are you traveling down the highway with a carload of kids and the noise is starting to get to you? Is it a rainy day and the kids are cooped up inside and need something to do? Well, give *these* a try!

What is the correct Arizona place name for the following?

1. A mythical bird
2. Above average
3. City leader
4. Table top in Spanish
5. Biblical dancer
6. No worries
7. Heroic nurse
8. Cupid saint
9. What you place on a grave
10. Vale of the skeletons
11. Christian holiday
12. House and Senate
13. Lack of señoritas
14. Twin male offspring
15. Too much protection
16. Elephant's early relative
17. Orb of male deer
18. The Baptist
19. Edge of a body of water
20. Male royalty
21. Falls in winter
22. Fits new suits
23. Uppermost part of tree
24. Royal servant
25. Spherical map
26. Mr. Franklin's son
27. What you get when you slide into a base
28. The complete stream
29. Sitting in a stream milking a cow
30. General MacArthur
31. Two heads are better than one
32. Caught off guard
33. Contradictory place name of bloody feud
34. A big house
35. What a vendor does
36. Holds a patriotic banner
37. Writer Tennessee _____
38. Fire residue and eating utensil
39. Not much breeze
40. Child's favorite question
41. Famous knife
42. Brilliant idea
43. Old Apache home
44. Type of desert plant used to make shampoo
45. On every old silver dollar
46. A kind of whiskey
47. Wise biblical king
48. City in Iraq
49. The Seer of Delphi
50. Musical team with Sullivan
51. To sell your poker chips
52. Defeated by Truman
53. Unbranded calf
54. Coronation
55. What we hope next year will be

56. What you do on allowance day
57. A bunch of agricultural enterprises
58. Another name for bedroom
59. A town full of brass instruments
60. A view of the mountains
61. A pair of pistols
62. A place of hot water
63. Recreation areas
64. Dizzy Dean's first name
65. A tree found along rivers
66. Also found in Ohio and Florida
67. Reach the heights
68. Great valley
69. Named for the garlic plant

Travel Trivia Locations

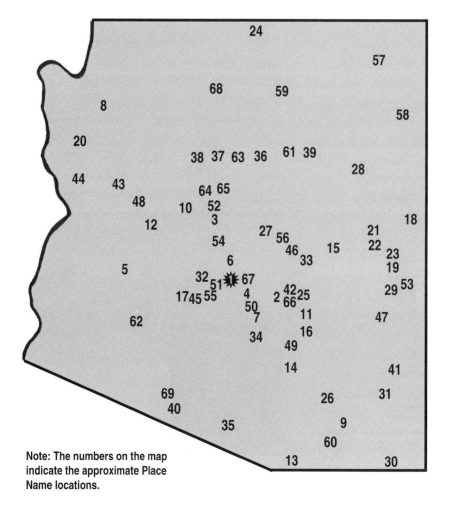

Note: The numbers on the map indicate the approximate Place Name locations.

Travel Trivia Answers

1. Phoenix
2. Superior
3. Mayer
4. Mesa
5. Salome
6. Carefree
7. Florence
8. Valentine
9. Tombstone
10. Skull Valley
11. Christmas
12. Congress
13. Nogales
14. Tucson
15. Overgaard
16. Mammoth
17. Buckeye
18. St. Johns
19. Lakeside
20. Kingman
21. Snowflake
22. Taylor
23. Pinetop
24. Page
25. Globe
26. Benson
27. Strawberry
28. Holbrook
29. Whiteriver
30. Douglas
31. Dos Cabezas
32. Surprise
33. Pleasant Valley
34. Casa Grande
35. Sells
36. Flagstaff
37. Williams
38. Ashfork
39. Winslow
40. Why
41. Bowie
42. Inspiration
43. Wikieup
44. Yucca
45. Liberty
46. Rye
47. Solomon
48. Bagdad
49. Oracle
50. Gilbert
51. Cashion
52. Dewey
53. Maverick
54. Crown King
55. Goodyear
56. Payson
57. Many Farms
58. Chambers
59. Tuba City
60. Sierra Vista
61. Two Guns
62. Agua Caliente
63. Parks
64. Jerome
65. Cottonwood
66. Miami
67. Pinnacle Peak
68. Grand Canyon
69. Ajo

Arizona Sports Trivia

*Arizona . . . a haven for sports
and for sportsmen!*

Sports has played an important role in Arizona since the days of the mining towns and military posts. Tombstone fielded a baseball team during the time when the Earp brothers were feuding with the Clantons and McLaury's. One of Geronimo's raids interrupted a baseball game. Holidays like the Fourth of July were highlighted by sports contests such as wrestling, boxing, drilling contests and baseball.

Arizona's mild climate encourages year around outdoor sports. In the middle of January, while the folks back in the Midwest are shoveling snow, Arizonans are enjoying a round of golf in their shirt sleeves, playing outdoor tennis, basketball or volleyball in shorts or participating in one of the ubiquitous winter softball or baseball programs.

The state's two largest institutions of higher learning, The **University of Arizona** and **Arizona State University** have enjoyed huge success in sports. The wide, open spaces and great climate have a very positive effect on recruiting. **Grand Canyon University**, located in Phoenix, has been a powerhouse in baseball and basketball almost since the beginning of its athletic programs in the mid-1950s. Again, the weather has been a major factor in that school's success.

Sports programs such as the one at ASU welcomed African-American student-athletes in the 1930s, long before they were accepted at many other colleges in the nation. Word got around and some of the country's greatest black athletes came to ASU. This went a long way towards making ASU a national power in college sports in the past 40 years.

Major league baseball arrived in Arizona in 1947 when **Bill Veeck**, colorful and innovative owner of the Cleveland Indians, decided to train in Tucson. Needing a second team, he convinced Horace Stoneham, owner of the New York Giants, to train in Phoenix. A few years later, the Cubs opened in Mesa, the Orioles moved to Scottsdale and the **Cactus League** was born. In 1927, **Babe Ruth** had given Arizonans their first glimpse of Major League Baseball when he stepped off a passenger train at the Phoenix depot and hit a few baseballs for the crowd that had gathered.

Other major league sports have arrived only recently. The

Phoenix Suns opened play in 1968 and the **Arizona Cardinals** arrived in 1988. In 1995, Arizona received a major-league baseball franchise, the **Arizona Diamondbacks.**

Back in the days before major league baseball, basketball and football, and before ASU and the UofA became national sports powers, Class C baseball, semi-pro baseball and fast pitch softball dominated the sports pages of Arizona's newspapers. This writer played for the semi-pro Glendale Greys in 1956 when they battled the perennial state champion, Casa Grande Cotton Kings, for the Arizona State Semi-pro Championship.

In Phoenix, fast pitch softball teams used to draw 7,000 fans when the population of the city was only around 60,000. Men's teams like the Lettuce Kings and Funk Jewelers, along with women's teams, A1 Queens and PBSW Ramblers, won several national championships during the 1930s, 40s and 50s. Athletes like **Dot Wilkinson, Charlotte "Skipper" Armstrong, Dodie Nelson, Carolyn Morris, Paul "Windmill" Watson, "Wimpy" Jones, Jay Bob Bickford, "Nolly" Trujillo, Al Linde, Jerry Wells** and the husband-wife pitching combination of **Margie** and **Kenny Law** were local legends on the Arizona sports scene.

Charlotte "Skipper" Armstrong is listed in *The Guinness Book of Records* and *Ripley's Believe It Or Not* for a strong pitching performance in 1945, while hurling for the South Bend Blue Sox in the All-American Girls Professional Baseball League. She was memorialized in the recent film *A League of Their Own*. Skipper pitched both ends of a double-header. One game went 15 innings and the other 17 innings. She threw shutouts in both games. Armstrong, who became a professional ballplayer while she was still a Phoenix high school student, was later a 5-time All-American for the Phoenix A1 Queens.

Margie Law was the only player to win All-American honors at three positions: pitcher, outfield and first base. Husband Kenny was most valuable player in the national championships in 1948. A year later he struck out 79 batters, a record that still stands, on his way to being named top pitcher in the tourney.

Dot Wilkinson was the best woman athlete in Arizona history. She began her professional career with the Ramblers while still in her early teens. She was selected to the All-American team an amazing 19 times. Wilkinson was later a national champion bowler.

From 1945 to 1957, games were played at the Phoenix Softball Park at 15th Avenue and Roosevelt. During a season, 150,000 fans filled the ballparks to see these athletes perform. In 1948, 279,000 fans came out to watch the A1 Queens play across the United States and Canada. The team, coached by Larry Walker, reached the national finals or semifinals 12 of 13 years. One of his players was former Arizona governor, **Rose Mofford.**

With the exception of a few movie theaters in downtown Phoenix, there was little else to do for leisure activity but head out to the ballpark. During the 1950s, television and air conditioning sent the leagues into steady decline. The old ballparks are gone and the noise of the crowd has faded, but for those, this writer included, who watched players like Margie Law, Dot Wilkinson and Skipper Armstrong grace the diamond, their feats are indelibly etched in our memories.

The Arizona contingent of the old Class C Arizona-Texas League consisted of the Tucson Cowboys, Phoenix Senators, Globe-Miami Browns and Bisbee-Douglas Copper Kings. Between games they rode hot buses along desert highways, hanging their uniforms and underwear out the windows to dry, and slept in cheap hotels. They played in towns like Mexicali, Cananea, El Paso and Juarez where baseball wasn't just a game—it was a religion. Billy Martin played his first professional season with the Phoenix Senators. Alex Kellner and Corky Reddell had great careers with the Tucson Cowboys. One glorious season Reddell won 28 games. Kellner went on to pitch for Connie Mack's Philadelphia Athletics.

1995 was a banner year for sports in Arizona. The NBA played its All-Star game in the new **America West Arena** in Phoenix and Major League Baseball awarded a franchise to the Arizona Diamondbacks. **Phoenix Suns** majority owner **Jerry Colangelo** is the Diamondbacks owner and former New York Yankee manager, **Buck Showalter**, is the team's first manager. The **Winnipeg Jets** of the National Hockey League are re-locating to Phoenix where they will play their home games (starting with the 1996-1997 season) in America West Arena and be known as the **Coyotes**; the Phoenix Suns reached the semi-finals of the Western Conference before losing to the eventual champion Houston Rockets; the inaugural **World Championship of Golf**, which offered a record $1 million first prize was held in the Valley and **Sun Devil Stadium** hosted the **Fiesta Bowl**, in which Nebraska came up the winner over the Florida Gators.

Arizona really hit the big time as a major league sports town on January 18, 1996 when ASU and the City of Tempe hosted **Super Bowl XXX**. The game was the most-watched television event in history and the game between Pittsburgh and Dallas lived up to the Super Bowl hype. It was too close to call until the last four minutes when Dallas scored to ice the victory at 27-17.

That same weekend the **Phoenix Open** was won by **Phil Mickelson**, a former golf star at ASU.

General Sports Trivia

Some of these questions will be easy for the typical sports fan. Others will challenge even the most avid radio sports-talk enthusiast. Let's see how well you know your Arizona sports history.

1. What was the team name of the old Arizona-Texas League representing Globe-Miami during the 1940s-50s?

2. What were the names of Phoenix, Arizona's two leading women's professional softball teams during the 1930s, 40s and 50s?

3. Name the 1956 World Series Yankee hero who hurled in the old Arizona-Texas League with the Globe-Miami team.

4. What was the name of the Phoenix team in the old Class C Arizona-Texas League?

5. Name the controversial ballplayer-manager whose professional career began with Phoenix in the Class C Arizona-Texas League in 1947.

6. What was Tucson's name in the Arizona-Texas League?

7. In 1953, this Scottsdale athlete won an amazing 28 games pitching for Tucson and was the toast of the Arizona-Texas League. Who was he?

8. Bisbee-Douglas also had a team in the Arizona-Texas League. What was their name?

9. Name the great woman athlete who captained and caught for the PBSW Ramblers during the 1940s-50s. She played in 27 national tournaments and was All-American 19 times. She was also a champion bowler.

10. Name the star pitcher for the Funk Jewelers in 1930s fast pitch softball who was later governor and U.S. Senator.

11. Name two players on the 1995-1996 NBA World Champion Chicago Bulls team who formerly starred for the UofA Wildcats.

12. Who was *RING Magazine's* 1993 Fighter of the Year?

13. Name the former Major League Baseball star, who is a native of Williams.

14. Name the first two teams to play in the Fiesta Bowl, 1971.

15. Name the rodeo cowboy from Gilbert who teamed up with

Jake Barnes to win a record 5 straight PRCA team roping championships (1985-1989). They also won in 1992 & 1994.

16. Name the first African-American to win a PRCA bull-riding championship in 1982.

17. Who won Tucson's first Copper Bowl (1989)?

18. Name the only person to win an Academy Award as well as a Professional World Cowboy championship.

19. Name the ASU track coach who put ASU on the map in the 1950s, 60s & 70s. He coached 60 individual champions, 10 NCAA champions and 34 All-Americans. In 1977 he won the NCAA track championship.

20. Who was the first Phoenix pro player to make baseball's Hall of Fame?

21. What country music stars performed the first show at the America West Arena?

22. Name the Mesa High School athlete and Los Angeles Dodger who was the surprise hero of the 1988 World Series.

23. Name the bronc rider from Phoenix who is the PRCA All-Around Cowboy 1989-1994, six consecutive times.

24. Name the 1978 Fiesta Bowl Queen.

25. Who coached the UofA basketball team from 1972-82 and was the first African-American to head a NCAA Div. 1 Basketball program.

26. Who defeated Michigan in the 1987 Rose Bowl?

27. Name teams going for national championship at the Fiesta Bowl in 1987.

28. Which Arizona team appeared in Arizona's first Salad Bowl, at Montgomery Stadium in 1949?

29. Name the 1992, PRCA Bullriding Champ.

30. Name the great softball pitcher for the PBSW Ramblers during the 1940s-50s. She was later on the faculty at ASU.

31. Name this left-handed pitcher for the A1 Queens who became the first African-American woman inducted into the National Softball Hall of Fame.

32. Name the long-time coach and promoter of the A1 Queens. He also founded and still runs the Basketball Congress International.

33. Name the legendary men's softball pitcher who, in the 1949 national tournament, struck out 79 batters.

34. Name the first team from Arizona to win a professional sports world's championship.

35. Who was the coach of that team (see #34)?

36. The first native-born Arizona woman to run track and field in the Olympics (1968) was _____?

37. Name the Arizona high school with the longest football winning streak as of November, 1995.

38. Name this Arizona resident who, in 1977, was the first man to break the 200 mph speed barrier at the Indianapolis Speedway. He also won the race in 1983. In 1980 he started in last place and finished second for the biggest advance in Indy history.

39. Name this Arizona resident who was the first African-American pitcher to win a World Series game.

40. Name this Arizona legend in the ranks of coaching Olympic diving champions. He coached several Olympic teams both for the U.S. and foreign countries.

41. What annual New Year's bowl game, sponsored by the Phoenix Kiwanis Club, was played in Montgomery Stadium (1940's and 1950's)?

42. Who was the first Arizona high school basketball player to be named First Team All-American?

43. Who is the only golfer to win three straight Phoenix Opens?

44. Name the Phoenix Suns' first coach.

45. What college's team name is the "Artichokes"?

46. Name 1 of the 2 professional football teams that preceded the Arizona Cardinals.

47. Name the Tucson High pitcher who won 20 games as a rookie for Connie Mack's Philadelphia Athletics in 1949.

48. Before they became the Thunderbirds, what were Mesa Community College's athletic teams called?

49. To which football conference does Northern Arizona University belong?

50. This resident of Tucson was from a famous rodeo family that included her brother, "Turk" and sister, "Montana

Red." All three were world champion bronc riders in the 1930s and 40s. She was the first woman inducted into the American Cowgirl Hall of Fame and is also in the National Cowboy Hall of Fame (see photo page 104).

51. Name the Arizona boxer who won a silver medal in the 1988 Olympics.

52. Name the Scottsdale High School all-state baseball athlete and three time Cy Young winner who pitched for the Baltimore Orioles.

53. Name the Arizonan who won the 1958 Indianapolis 500.

54. What well-known Arizona politician played basketball for the Denver Nuggets?

55. In 1989, where was the first Copper Bowl played?

56. Where are the University of Arizona's home basketball games played?

57. Name the football bowl game where ASU alumni played UofA alumni in Phoenix.

58. Who owns and operates the Sunrise Ski Area?

59. Name one major horseracing track in Arizona.

60. What are Arizona's two AAA minor-league baseball teams?

61. Who was the coach of the Phoenix Cardinals when they first moved to Arizona from St Louis?

62. At what school are "Lumberjacks" found?

63. Who won the first Fiesta Bowl?

64. What Hall of Fame baseball player spent his rookie spring training in Phoenix with the New York Yankees in 1951?

65. Name the only Arizona baseball player to play on a national champion junior college, NCAA and world champion major league team.

66. Name the golf course where the Phoenix Open is played.

67. Name the top heavyweight boxing contender from Chandler who fought Muhammad Ali for the world championship in 1967.

68. Name the Arizona-Texas league 1940s pitcher who in 1955 pitched the only perfect game in a World Series.

69. Name the "Happy Hopi from Shungopovi" who ran the marathon in the 1908 Olympics and won a silver medal in

the 10,000 meters in 1912.

70. Name the largest wood-supported dome stadium in the world. (Give proper name.)

71. What outstanding Phoenix-area softball player later became a governor and U.S. senator?

72. What did Arnold Palmer, Jack Nicklaus and Barry Goldwater all accomplish?

73. Name the only baseball coach who won national championships at all 3 levels: American Legion, Community College and NCAA.

74. Who was the only Arizonan to hit four home runs in a major league baseball game?

75. Name the mascot of the all-black Phoenix Carver High School.

76. Who won the 1981 Fiesta Bowl?

77. Who was the only Arizona high school football player to play on 4 consecutive State championship teams?

78. Who was the first Arizonan to play in the NFL?

79. What do the initials of the Arizona horse group A.T.B.A. stand for?

80. What was the first televised sports event in Arizona history?

81. Name one downhill ski area in Arizona.

82. Name the boxer from Globe who was the first Arizona native to win a world boxing title.

83. Who hit the first baseball out of Phoenix Municipal Stadium?

84. What resort has the Blue, Gold and West golf courses?

85. Who is the first Arizona coach inducted into the College Football Hall of Fame?

86. What nationally-known golf clubs are manufactured in Phoenix?

87. Name the quarterback and fullback on the 1945 Tucson High School football team that still holds the record for consecutive wins (1942-46) with 32.

88. Name this Scottsdale artist who was a 5-time All-American pitcher for the A 1 Queens. She is in *Ripley's Believe It Or Not* and *The Guinness Book of Records*. *(See photo page 104)*

89. Name the band from Arizona that performed the National Anthem at the National Football League's first Super Bowl in Los Angeles in 1967.

90. Name the two teams in Super Bowl XXX at ASU in 1996.

91. What was the final score in Super Bowl XXX at ASU?

92. Name the Most Valuable Player in Super Bowl XXX.

93. The Super Bowl XXX in Arizona on January 18, 1996 marked the tenth anniversary of what tragic event in American history?

94. Name the two teams competing for the national championship in the 1996 Fiesta Bowl.

95. Name the former ASU star who won the 1996 Phoenix Open.

96. Who arrived in the Salt River Valley in the Spring of 1994 and proclaimed, "You've got a winner in town!"?

97. He left town two years later. What was his record?

98. Name the two university coaches who perform the zany commercials on television for Bank One.

99. Rex Ellsworth, scion of an old Arizona family, owned a race horse that won the Kentucky Derby in 1955. Name that horse.

100. Who scored the first touchdown in Super Bowl XXX?

101. Name the boxer from Glendale who fought for the world title seven times in the welterweight and middleweight divisions during the 1940's and 50's. Marty Robbins also used his name in a popular country song in the 1950's.

102. Name the Phoenix-born swimmer who won 3 gold and 1 silver medal in the 1968 Olympics. Hint: His brother Tom (both swam for Indiana University) had the world's fastest time in the 100 Meter Freestyle in 1974.

103. Name the Phoenix-born Olympic swimmer who won the Silver Medal in 1968 in the 400 Individual Medley, the Silver Medal in 1972 in the 200 Butterfly and in 1976 the Bronze Medal in the 100 Butterfly. In 1981 he was inducted into the International Swimming Hall of Fame. Today he is a prominent Phoenix eye surgeon.

104. Name the Olympic diver from Mesa who was in both the 1960 and 1964 Olympics. In the 1964 Tokyo games she won a Bronze medal in the Three Meter competition.

105. Name the Arizona swimmer who anchored the Gold Medal-winning U.S. Mens 4 x 100 Freestyle and the 4 x 100 Medley relay teams at the Centennial Olympics at Atlanta. (The team set an Olympic record of 3:15.41 in the freestyle event.)

106. Name the Arizona gymnast who led the U.S. women's gymnastic team to its first Gold Medal at the Centennial Olympics. She courageously completed her event despite a severe ankle injury.

Charlotte "Skipper" Armstrong—of Scottsdale was a 5-time All-American pitcher for the A1 Queens. She is listed in *Ripley's Believe It Or Not* and *The Guinness Book of Records.*

(Photo courtesy Arizona Historical Foundation)

Alice Greenaugh—Is the first woman inducted into the American Cowgirl Hall of Fame and is also in the National Cowboy Hall of Fame.

(Photo courtesy Southwest Studies, Maricopa Community College)

Sports in General Answers

1. Globe-Miami Browns
2. A1 Queens and PBSW Ramblers
3. Don Larson. (He pitched the only perfect game in World Series history).
4. Phoenix Senators
5. Billy Martin
6. Tucson Cowboys
7. Corky Reddell
8. Bisbee-Douglas Copper Kings
9. Dot Wilkinson
10. Paul Fannin
11. Steve Kerr & Jud Buechler
12. Michael Carbajal
13. Billy Hatcher
14. ASU vs Florida State
15. Clay O'Brian Cooper
16. Charlie Sampson, who lives in Casa Grande
17. UofA over North Carolina State 17-10
18. Ben Johnson
19. Senon "Baldy" Castillo
20. Willie McCovey (Phoenix Giants, PCL 1958.)
21. George Strait and Pam Tillis (June, 1992)
22. Mickey Hatcher
23. Ty Murray
24. Channel 12's Jineane Ford
25. Fred Snowden
26. ASU
27. Penn State and Miami.
28. The University of Arizona. They lost to Drake, 14-3
29. Cody Custer of Wickenburg
30. Margie Law
31. Billie Harris
32. Larry Walker
33. Kenny Law
34. Arizona Rattlers. They beat Orlando 36-31 in Arena Bowl VIII (1994).
35. Danny White
36. Lois Anne Drinkwater. The seventeen-year-old ran in the 400 Meter in Mexico City. She was in lane one of the semi-finals. The lane was flooded and cost her a chance to win.
37. St. Johns Redskins with 42 consecutive wins as of November, 1995.
38. Tom Sneva
39. Joe Black, Brooklyn Dodgers, 1952, versus Yankees
40. Dick Smith
41. Salad Bowl (1940s and 1950s)
42. Sean Elliott, UofA, 1988 and 1989
43. Arnold Palmer
44. Johnny "Red" Kerr
45. Scottsdale Community College
46. Arizona Wranglers and Arizona Outlaws
47. Alex Kellner
48. Hokams, as in Hohokams
49. Big Sky Conference
50. Alice Greenough
51. Michael Carbajal
52. Jim Palmer
53. Jimmy Bryan
54. "Mo" Udall
55. Tucson, Arizona Stadium
56. McKale Center
57. Goulash Bowl
58. White Mtn. Apache Tribe

59. Turf Paradise, Prescott Downs and Rillito Downs
60. The Phoenix Firebirds and the Tucson Toros
61. Gene Stallings
62. NAU
63. ASU
64. Mickey Mantle
65. Gary Gentry
66. Scottsdale TPC Course
67. Zora Folley
68. Don Larson (New York Yankees)
69. Lewis Tewanima
70. J. Lawrence Walkup Skydome at NAU
71. Paul Fannin
72. All have won the Phoenix Open (Goldwater in 1934)
73. Jim Brock, ASU
74. Bob Horner - Atlanta Braves
75. Monarchs
76. Nobody. The day of the game was changed to January 1, so no game was played in 1981.
77. George Greathouse
78. Cecil Mulleneaux of ASC at Flagstaff. (He played for the New York Giants from 1932 to 1941)
79. Arizona Thoroughbred Breeders Association (Phoenix)
80. The Salad Bowl between Arizona State College at Tempe and Xavier of Ohio in 1950 (Xavier won 33-21)
81. Sunrise, Snow Bowl, Mt. Lemmon, Williams and Greer
82. Louis Espinoza (WBA Jr. Featherweight/1987)
83. Willie Mays (1964)
84. The Wigwam
85. Dan Devine
86. PING™ Golf Clubs
87. Frank Borman, quarterback, and Karl Eller, fullback
88. Charlotte "Skipper" Armstrong
89. The University of Arizona Marching Band
90. The Dallas Cowboys and the Pittsburgh Steelers
91. Dallas over Pittsburg, 27-17
92. Dallas defensive back Larry Brown. He had 2 interceptions that led to two Dallas touchdowns providing the margin of victory.
93. The Space Shuttle Challenger exploded after takeoff in 1986.
94. Nebraska Cornhuskers and the Florida Gators
95. Phil Mickelson
96. Buddy Ryan
97. 12 wins and 20 losses
98. Bill Freider, ASU and Lute Olson, UofA
99. Swaps
100. Former Arizona Cardinal, Jay Novacek.
101. Jimmy Martinez
102. Charlie Hickcox
103. Gary Hall, Sr. (his son Gary Hall, Jr. was a 1996 Olympian.)
104. Patsy Willard
105. Gary Hall, Jr. (He also won Silver Medals in the men's 50 and 100 Freestyle.
106. Kerri Strug (The Russians had dominated this event for four decades before Kerri and her teammates brought the gold to America.)

University of Arizona Sports Trivia

University of Arizona General Sports

1. Name the Arizona student body president and athlete who provided their slogan, "Bear Down," while he lay dying from an auto accident in 1926.

2. His dying words, "...tell them...tell them to bear down...," were passed on to his teammates that day by coach "Pop" McKale and thus inspired they went on to defeat whom?

3. What were the original colors of the University of Arizona? (before Cardinal and Navy)

4. Why were they changed to Cardinal and Navy?

5. How did the University acquire its nickname, "Wildcats"?

6. Up to that time what were the teams called?

7. What is the trophy retained by the winner in the Arizona-New Mexico rivalry?

8. What frontier legend allegedly owned this Springfield rifle? Hint: It wasn't Carson.

9. What is the name of the Wildcat fight song?

10. What is the other name for "A" Mountain in Tucson?

11. A charter member of the Arizona Sports Hall of Fame, he was coach and athletic director at the University from 1914 to 1957. Who was he?

12. What is the name of the Wildcat marching band?

13. In what sport did the Wildcats win NCAA championships in 1991, 1993, 1994 and 1996 (they were runner-up in both 1992 and 1995)?

14. Name this coach. For the past decade he's coached softball at the UofA. Earlier, he won two National Junior College championships in five seasons at Central Arizona Community College. In 1994, the Wildcats played in their 7th straight College World Series. It's worth mentioning: The 1994 team (64-3) placed 6 players first-team All-American. They also set NCAA records for victories (64), home runs (93), runs (527) and hits (701). In the 1994

College World Series, the Wildcats outscored their opponents 38-2.

15. Name the former Scottsdale Chaparral High School softball pitcher who led the Wildcats to 3 NCAA Women's Softball Championships in 1991 and 1993, and 1994. Her career record was 101 wins and 9 losses. In career World Series play she had 9 wins, and gave up only 2 earned runs in 97 innings. She finished the 1994 regular season with a 33-1 record. During her career she pitched 8 no-hitters, made first team All-American and was 1994 National Player of the Year.

16. Name the Wildcat softball slugger who hit a NCAA record 28 home runs in 1994, set a new record for career home runs with 46 while only a junior. In her senior year, hit 33 more home runs during the season and set a new NCAA record for career.

17. The UofA Wildcats Women's Softball team won a College World Series in 1996. Name another UofA team that also won a college championship that same month.

18. What is the name of UofA's football mascot? (Be specific)

19. In what sport did the UofA first gain national athletic recognition?

20. What football conference did ASU and UofA belong to prior to the WAC and PAC?

21. Who designed the UofA Wildcat mascot?

22. What well-known Arizonan was a basketball star at the UofA and the student body president as well?

23. Where did the brothers Udall, Mo and Stewart, Wildcat basketball stars during the 1940's, play their high school basketball?

24. Who was the "Grand Old Man" of Wildcat sports?

25. Name the prominant Arizona politician who was a member of the 1928-1929 Wildcat swim team.

26. Name the Wildcat's first African-American basketball player.

University of Arizona Basketball

1. Name the first UofA player to have his basketball jersey retired.

2. How many times have the Wildcats reached the Final Four?

3. He starred for the Wildcats in 1942, 1947-48, but he's better remembered for his political career. Who is he?

4. Who were the two backcourt phenomenons who led the Wildcats to the Final Four in 1994.

5. Team USA won a gold medal at the World University Games in 1993. Name the Wildcat who captained that team.

6. Name the coach who has guided the Wildcats to 7 PAC-10 titles in the past 9 years (as of 1996).

7. The Wildcats 1987-92 home-court winning streak is one of the NCAA's top ten all-time. How many games in a row did they win at home?

8. The Wildcat teams from 1945-51 did even better, ranking 6th among the top ten all-time NCAA home-court winning streaks. How many home games in a row did they win?

9. The 1988 Wildcats put together their finest season in history. What was their record?

10. Where do the Wildcats play their home games?

11. Where did they play their home games before 1973?

12. Who holds the Wildcat season scoring record?

13. Who holds the Wildcat career scoring record?

14. Who holds the Wildcat game high scoring record?

15. Name this Wildcat who led the team in steals for three years (1986-89) and assists one year (1988-89), who became a star baseball player for the Cleveland Indians.

16. Name this popular Wildcat who, on the 1985-86 PAC-10 Championship squad, led the team in assists, field goal percentage, free throw percentage, steals and was PAC-10 All-Academic.

17. Name the Wildcat who was the 1990 National Player of the Year.

18. What NBA award did former Wildcat Damon Stoudamire win in 1996?

University of Arizona
Football

1. Name the legendary coach and athletic director who has a center named for him on the campus.

2. What is the annual prize awarded the victor in the Arizona-Arizona State game?

3. Prior to 1979, what was the annual prize awarded the victor in the Arizona-Arizona State game?

4. The Wildcats appeared in bowl games in 1921, 1949, 1968, 1979, 1985 and 1986. What was significant about the 1986 bowl game?

5. January 1, 1994, was a first for the Wildcats. Name it.

6. Which bowl game did the Wildcats win in 1994?

7. Who did they defeat in that game?

8. Who was Most Valuable Player in the 1994 Fiesta Bowl?

9. Who was Most Valuable Player in the 1992 Hancock Bowl in El Paso?

10. Who holds the Wildcat career interception record?

11. Which 1950s Wildcat was known as the "Cactus Comet?"

12. Who holds the Wildcat rushing record for touchdowns scored in a game (5); a season (21); and a career (44)?

13. Who holds the Wildcat record for most touchdown passes in a career?

14. Who holds the Wildcat record for most points scored in a game, 32; in a season, 166?

15. Who holds the Wildcat record for most points scored in a career?

16. Who is the all-time rushing leader for the Wildcats? He also holds the all-time single game rushing record, 1,359 yds.

17. Ricky Hunley, Rob Waldrop, Chuck Cecil and Tedy Bruschi share an honor. What is it?

18. Who was the first Wildcat to be named to any All-American team?

19. Chuck Cecil made another All-American team 3 years running. Which team was it?

20. Name the two Wildcats who played in recent Super Bowls with the Buffalo Bills.

21. The 1993 Wildcats had their finest season in the history of the University, dating back to 1899. What was their record?

22. Name this flamboyant receiver, former Wildcat, who also played for the Denver Broncos in recent Super Bowl history. Hint: He also won the NCAA long jump championship.

23. Another two-sport athlete running back and two-time PAC 10 sprint king before winning a bronze medal in the 200 meter race at Barcelona in 1990. Name him.

24. Name this Wildcat who won the 1990 Jim Thorpe Award as the nation's best defensive back.

25. Chuck Cecil's unforgettable "Miracle Run" interception (1986—UofA vs. ASU) covered how many yards?

26. Name the Wildcat star of the 1969 season who played in the Super Bowl for the Baltimore Colts the following season.

27. Name this former All-American, All-Pro, Arizona native who also coached the Wildcats. He played on two Green Bay Packer championship teams in 1938 and 1941 and was All-Pro twice. He and his brother, Cecil, were the first two Arizonans to play professional football.

28. Name the outstanding Mesa High School athlete who was a star running back for the Wildcats and later played several years as a defensive back for the Dallas Cowboys.

29. Eddie Wilson, Bobby Lee Thompson and Joe Hernandez made up the backfield of the 1961, 8-1-1 Wildcats. Because of several dramatic last-second comebacks, they were dubbed the....?

30. Who was the coach of the 1961 Wildcat football team?

31. Rodney Peete starred for the University of Southern California and later played in the NFL. His father was a star athlete at Mesa High School and the University of Arizona. He was for many years an assistant football coach for the Wildcats. Who was he?

University of Arizona Baseball

1. Name this all-around athlete who starred in football, basketball and baseball, 1929-31. He is a member of the Arizona Sports Hall of Fame and following his career as a Wildcat, was a slugging star for the New York Giants in the National League.

2. The Wildcat's legendary baseball coach from 1950-72. He is also a charter member of the Arizona Sports Hall of Fame and a ballpark is named for him. Who is he?

3. What was significant about the 1976 Wildcat baseball team?

4. Which other Wildcat teams won a NCAA College World Series?

5. What is so unique and persevering of these three national champion teams?

6. Name the illustrious Wildcat baseball coach who retired in 1996. He has won more than 800 games over a 22-year span, was inducted into the American Baseball Coaches Association Hall of Fame in 1990, has won three national titles and has been National Coach of the Year three times. As a player, he led his Minnesota team to the College World Series title in 1956 and is the only person to play for and coach a national champion. He also played eight years in the major leagues.

7. The 1956 Wildcats featured two of the best pitchers in collegiate baseball that year. Who were they?

8. Name the top two Wildcat pitchers for career wins.

9. Who was the NCAA Most Valuable Player in 1980 on the national champion Wildcat team?

10. Ron Hassey, Hank Leiber, Eddie Leon, Joe Magrane, Dave Stegman, Don Lee, Carl Thomas, Terry Francona and Craig Lefferts all share career achievements. What do they have in common?

University of Arizona
Sports Trivia Answers

GENERAL

1. John "Button" Salmon
2. New Mexico 7-0
3. Sage Green and Silver
4. In 1899, the student manager of the football team was able to strike a bargain on purchasing game sweaters. The sweaters were blue, trimmed in red. So he formally requested the colors be changed to fit and his request was approved.
5. In 1914, a *Los Angeles Times* student correspondent, Bill Henry, who was covering the Arizona-Occidental game wrote: "The Arizona men showed the fight of wildcats." The Arizona student body quickly voted to change their name.
6. Varsity
7. The Kit Carson Rifle
8. Geronimo
9. "Bear Down Arizona"
10. Sentinel Peak
11. James F. "Pop" McKale
12. The *"Pride of Arizona"*
13. Arizona Women's Softball
14. Mike Candera
15. Susie Parra
16. Laura Espinoza
17. Women's Golf team
18. Wilbur the Wildcat
19. Polo
20. Border Conference
21. Kearney Egerton, longtime writer and cartoonist at the

Arizona Republic
22. Morris "Mo" Udall
23. St Johns High School
24. J. F. "Pop" McKale. He coached Wildcat teams for nearly fifty years.
25. Barry Goldwater
26. Hadie Redd, who played high school ball at Phoenix Carver High School

BASKETBALL

1. Sean Elliott (#32)
2. Twice. (1988 and 1994)
3. Morris "Mo" Udall
4. Khalid Reeves and Damon Stoudamire
5. Damon Stoudamire
6. Lute Olson. (1986, 1988 through 1991, 1993 and 1994.)
7. 71
8. 81
9. 35 wins and 3 losses
10. McKale Memorial Center
11. Bear Down Gym
12. Sean Elliott, 743. (1987-88)
13. Sean Elliott, 2555. (1985-89)
14. Ernie McCray, 46. (1960)
15. Ken Lofton
16. Steve Kerr
17. Sean Elliott
18. Rookie of the Year

FOOTBALL

1. J. F. "Pop" McKale (McKale Memorial Center)
2. Big Game Trophy (since 1979)
3. The Governor's Trophy (The official state flag of Arizona)

4. They won their first bowl game, the Aloha Bowl, defeating North Carolina, 30-21

5. They played in a New Year's bowl game for the first time. They also shared their first-ever PAC 10 title.

6. Fiesta Bowl in Tempe

7. The Wildcats demolished highly touted Miami 29-0.

8. All around athlete, Chuck Levy

9. All-American Rob Waldrop of the Wildcats

10. Chuck Cecil, 21 interceptions (also a PAC 10 record)

11. Art Lupino (1953-56)

12. Art Lupino (1954)

13. Tom Tunnicliffe, 46 (1980-83)

14. Art Lupino (1954)

15. Max Zendejas, 360 points. (1982-85)

16. Art Lupino, 3,371 yards (1953-56)

17. All three were named to the Consensus All-American 1st Team

18. Fred Enke Jr. (1947) AP 3rd team

19. Academic All-American

20. Glenn Parker and John Fina

21. 10 wins 2 losses. Including a smashing 28-0 thrashing of the Miami Hurricanes in the Fiesta Bowl.

22. Vance Johnson

23. Michael Bates

24. Darryll Lewis

25. 103 yards

26. Ron Gardin

27. Carl "Moose" Mulleneaux

28. Warren Livingston

29. "Cardiac Kids." Among their victories was an upset of Arizona State and a tie with Nebraska.

30. Jim LaRue

31. Willie Peete

BASEBALL

1. Hank Leiber

2. Frank Sancet

3. They won their first NCAA College World Series.

4. 1980 and 1986

5. They came up through the loser's bracket each time to win it all.

6. Jerry Kindall (1973-1996)

7. Don Lee 15-0 and Carl Thomas 14-3

8. Don Lee 36-7 (1954-56) and Carl Thomas 35-5 (1954-56)

9. Terry Francona, who later starred in the major leagues

10. All reached the "Show" or the major leagues and all are in the Arizona Sports Hall of Fame.

Jerry Kindall — UofA baseball coach (1973-1996)

Lute Olson — UofA basketball coach who has guided the Wildcats to 7 PAC-10 titles in the past 9 years (as of 1996).

Sean Elliott — UofA basketball star who was the first to have his jersey retired. He holds the Wildcat season and career scoring records.

(Above Left) **Steve Kerr** — UofA basketball star who led the Wildcats to the 1985-86 PAC-10 Championship. He was named PAC-10 All-Academic that same year.

(Above Center) **Chuck Levy** — UofA football MVP of the 1994 Fiesta bowl.

(Above Right) **Susie Parra** — UofA softball pitcher who led the Wild-cats to 3 NCAA Women's Softball Championships (1991, 1993, 1994)

All UofA Photos courtesy UofA Sports Department

Arizona State University Sports Trivia

Arizona State University Basketball

1. The 1962-63 ASU basketball team finished third in the nation and was, perhaps, the greatest basketball team ever assembled at Tempe. Who was the coach of that team?

2. Which power player on that 1962-63 "Dream Team" was known as "The Horse"?

3. Name the tall, sharpshooting center on the amazing 1962-63 team (26-3) who later played professional ball in the American Basketball Association.

4. Who was "Jumping Joe" on the 1962-63 team? He later played in the NBA.

5. Name this Sun Devil great. He played at ASU 1974-75, and won an NBA championship with the Portland Trailblazers in 1977.

6. Name this legendary basketball coach who won 406 games for ASU and in his career, won more than 500 games (including exhibitions).

7. Who holds the single-game high score record for the Sun Devil basketball team in the University Activity Center? Hint: He was a first-round draft pick by Portland in 1982. He later starred for the Denver Nuggets.

8. Who was the only Sun Devil basketball player to be named all-conference for three seasons?

9. Only one Sun Devil basketball player has played for the U.S. in the Olympic games. Name that player.

10. Who is ASU's only first team All-American basketball player?

11. Who holds the Sun Devil basketball record for free throws, set from 1955-58. Hint: He's a well-known boys basketball coach in the Phoenix-area.

12. Name the Navajo woman basketball player who starred at Scottsdale Community College and Arizona State

University. During the 1992-93 season she led the PAC 10 in assists and was PAC 10 All-Conference. She was the only Native American representing the U.S. in the 1993 World University Games.

13. Bert Anthony, a cartoonist for Walt Disney, is best-remembered at ASU for what?

14. Name the former Sun Devil basketball coach who also coached and played baseball and football at the institution.

15. Who was ASU's opponent in its first recorded basketball game back in 1911?

16. Art Becker, Joe Caldwell, Tony Cerkvenik, Roy Coppinger, Tom Futch, Dave Graybill, Lionel Hollins, Lafayette Lever, Freddy Lewis and Byron Scott all share a unique honor. What is it?

17. What was ASU's team name before they became the "Sun Devils"?

18. What are the colors of ASU?

19. What is the nickname of the ASU Sun Devil mascot?

20. What ASU & Scottsdale Community College basketball star was inducted in the American Indian Athletic Hall of Fame?

 ## Arizona State University Football

1. What great football sports rivalry began in 1899?

2. Name the baseball player who came to ASU in the 1960s to play football.

3. Name the Westwood High School athlete who came to ASU to play baseball who later starred in football for the Dallas Cowboys.

4. Who was the coach of the undefeated 1957 Arizona State football team?

5. Who was Arizona State's first football coach in 1896?

6. Who was the first African-American to play varsity football at Arizona State?

7. Only two Sun Devil football players' jerseys have been permanently retired. Who were they? Hint: one played in the late 40s and early 50s. The other played in the mid-50s.

8. Who were the first Arizona State football players in the Super Bowl?

9. Name the running back from Mesa High who played for Arizona State in the late 40s. He later starred for the Chicago Bears and was known for his dazzling runs.

10. Who was the first Arizona State football player to play in the National Football League? Hint: It was way back in 1934.

11. Who was the All-American middle guard for Arizona State in the mid-60s, and was also the NCAA heavyweight wrestling champion in 1967? He later played for the Kansas City Chiefs and Houston Oilers.

12. Name this player who was a running back for Arizona State but was converted into a receiver by the Washington Redskins. He was NFL Rookie of the Year and held the NFL record for passes caught.

13. Which former governor was the Arizona State volunteer team doctor?

14. Which former governor was behind the microphone at radio station KOY in 1931 broadcasting the first Arizona State football game?

15. Name ASU's football training camp outside of Payson.

16. Name the Sun Devil quarterback '54, '55, '56 who also starred in baseball and basketball.

17. One of ASU's greatest football victories came in the Fiesta Bowl in 1975. They wound up No. 2 in the nation. Who did they defeat in that memorable bowl game?

18. Who was Arizona State's "first football star"? He's been immortalized in a school song and a sports dormitory was named for him. He played on the school's first football team back in 1896.

19. Name the legendary coach of the Arizona State Sun Devil football team who was a 175-pound All-American guard from Michigan State.

20. Who was the first consensus All-American football player at Arizona State University in 1972?

21. Name the quarterback in that same backfield who was named on several All-American first teams.

22. One of the greatest moments in Sun Devil football history came on January 1, 1987. What happened on that day?

23. Arguably, the best Sun Devil offensive line in Arizona State history was the 1987 Rose Bowl Championship team of Danny Villa, Randall McDaniel, Todd Kalis, and Kevin Thomas. Other than being a very talented group, what else was so unique about this group?

24. Who was the Most Valuable Player in the 1987 Rose Bowl game?

25. Which ASU quarterback holds the season record for passing?

26. Which ASU rusher holds the single-game rushing record? Hint: He hails from Eloy, Arizona and later starred in the NFL.

27. Who is ASU's all-time career leading rusher?

28. Who holds the ASU record for 100-yard-rushing games?

29. Who is the only ASU player to wear the number 33?

30. Name this ASU tailback who was the school's first three-time All-American and finished 8th in the Heisman Trophy voting in 1973.

31. Name this ASU kicker who, over a period of 3 seasons made 137 of 138 PAT attempts.

32. Who holds the record for the longest field goal in ASU history?

33. Who holds the ASU season record for net yards rushing?

34. "Whizzer" White shares the most career touchdowns, 48, with another ASU great; who is it?

35. Who holds the ASU record for most yards passing in a game?

36. Who holds the ASU record for most yards passing in a career?

37. Who holds the ASU record for most touchdown passes in a career?

38. Who holds the ASU record for career most total yards offense?

39. Who holds the ASU record for most yards advancing the ball, all fashions?

40. Name the two ASU football players who have gone on to be enshrined in the NFL Hall of Fame.

41. Name the ASU football coach elected to the College Hall of Fame.

 ## Arizona State University Baseball

1. Name the only Sun Devil pitcher to hurl a perfect game.

2. Name the former Sun Devil baseball player who has been the National League Most Valuable Player three times.

3. What do former coach Bobby Winkles and Oddibe McDowell have in common on the Sun Devil baseball team?

4. What did Reggie Jackson, Barry Bonds and Mike Kelly share on the Sun Devil baseball team?

5. Name the Sun Devil ballplayer who holds the record for a 45-game hitting streak set back in 1971. His .434 batting average was the highest until Paul LoDuca hit .446 in 1993.

6. Name the first Sun Devil baseball player to be an All-American and the first to make the major leagues.

7. Name the first ASU player taken in the first major league draft.

8. Sun Devil baseball alumni have appeared on the cover of *Sports Illustrated* 11 times. Ten of those were Reggie Jackson. Who was the eleventh?

9. Who was the Arizona State University baseball coach, 1959-71? He made the school a national power, won three national championships, '65, '67, '69, and later managed and coached in the major leagues.

10. Name the only coach to win national championships in American Legion baseball, (North Phoenix High); Junior

College, (Mesa Community College); and the NCAA, (ASU).

11. Name this former Sun Devil who once hit four homers in a major league game for the Atlanta Braves.

12. What do Sun Devil ballplayers, Rick Monday, Floyd Bannister and Bob Horner have in common?

13. What do Eddie Bane and Bob Horner have in common?

14. What do Jim Palmer, Robin Yount, Rick Sutcliffe, Dale Murphy, Gary Templeton and Billy Hatcher have in common?

15. Which former Sun Devil was a member of the 1969 "Amazing Mets"?

16. Which Sun Devil holds the record for home runs in a season?

17. Name the pitchers with the most victories in a season.

18. Sun Devil pitchers, John Pavlik '65, Craig Swan '69, Randy Newman '82 and Dave Graybill '84 all have something in common. What is it?

19. The most strikeouts recorded by a Sun Devil pitcher occurred in 1963 against Colorado State. This hurler struck out 22 hitters. Who was he?

20. Which Sun Devil pitcher(s) hold the record for career victories at ASU?

21. Name the only Sun Devil baseball player in major league baseball's Hall of Fame at Cooperstown, NY.

22. On April 7, 1974, the Sun Devils began playing baseball in their new stadium. What is the name of that stadium?

23. Who did the Sun Devils play in their first official baseball game in 1959?

24. Name the pitcher who holds the Sun Devil record for strikeouts in a season.

Arizona State University Sports

WOMEN'S GOLF

1. Name this woman golfer who ruled women's amateur golf in the 1950s and 60s. She became the first woman to earn a golf scholarship, won a record five U.S. Amateur crowns and was the top-ranked U.S. female golfer on five occasions. In 1982 she was inducted into the LPGA Hall of Fame.

MEN'S GOLF

1. Who was ASU's first four-time All-American in golf? He was the first golfer ever to win both the U.S. Public Links (1986) and U.S. Amateur (1987).

2. Name this three-time NCAA Medalist (1989, 1990, 1992) who won 16 individual tournaments for ASU. He is now a leading money winner on the PGA circuit.

WOMEN'S TENNIS

1. Name this legendary coach who headed the tennis program for thirty years. She was voted ITCA National Coach of the Year in 1984 and is a member of ASU's Hall of Distinction.

TRACK

1. Name this track coach who put Arizona State on the map during the 50s, 60s and 70s. He coached 60 individual champions, 10 NCAA champions and 34 All-Americans. In 1977 he won a national championship.

2. Mike Barrick, Henry Carr, Ron Freeman and Ulis Williams set a world record in 1963 in what event?

Arizona State University Sports Trivia Answers

BASKETBALL

1. Ned Wulk
2. Tony Cerkvenik. He holds the ASU career rebound record (1,022) and rebound average (12.3) (1960-1963).
3. Art Becker
4. Joe Caldwell
5. Lionel Hollins
6. Ned Wulk
7. Lafayette "Fat" Lever. 38 points vs. Arizona, Feb. 20, 1982. (Paul Williams holds the high score record with 45 vs. USC in 1983).
8. Joe Caldwell (1962,63,64)
9. Joe Caldwell (1964) (Alton Lister was a member of the 1980 team that boycotted the Olympics in Moscow.)
10. Lionel Hollins (1975)
11. Royce Youree
12. Ryneldi Becenti
13. In 1946, when the Bulldogs became the Sun Devils, he created "Sparky" the Sun Devil.
14. Bill Kajikawa
15. Mesa High.
16. They are the ten Sun Devil Basketball players in the ASU Hall of Fame.
17. Bulldogs
18. Maroon and gold
19. Sparky
20. Ryneldi Becenti

FOOTBALL

1. U of A vs. ASU (ASU won 11-2 but didn't defeat the Wild-cats or even score a point against the Wildcats again until 1931.)
2. Reggie Jackson
3. Danny White. In 40 games during the 1972 season, he hit .325 and hit 5 homers.
4. Dan Devine. (He later coached at Missouri, Notre Dame and the Green Bay Packers in the NFL.)
5. Fred Irish
6. Emerson Harvey, in 1937
7. Wilford "Whizzer" White #33 and Bobby Mulgado #27.
8. Danny White and Bob Bruenig, Dallas Cowboys, 1979. Both were Arizona high school products.
9. Wilford "Whizzer" White. (Father of Danny White.)
10. Norris Steverson of Mesa. He played for the Chicago Bears.
11. Curly Culp from Yuma.
12. Charley Taylor
13. Dr./Governor Ben Moeur
14. Governor Jack Williams
15. Camp Tontozona
16. Dave Graybill
17. Nebraska, 17-14
18. Charlie Haigler
19. Frank Kush
20. Woody Green. He went on to repeat the feat in 1973.
21. Danny White, who went on to quarterback the Dallas Cowboys.
22. The Sun Devils defeated Michigan 22-15 in the Rose Bowl.

23. All were from Arizona.
24. ASU quarterback Jeff Van Raaphorst
25. Danny White, 2,878 yards in 1973.
26. Ben Malone rushed for 250 yds. against Oregon State on October 27, 1973.
27. Woody Green, 4188 yds. (1971-72-73)
28. Woody Green, 25
29. Wilford "Whizzer" White
30. Woody Green
31. Luis Zendejas, 1981-84
32. Luis Zendejas, 55 yds. vs. Oregon State in 1982
33. Wilford "Whizzer" White, 1502 in 1950 in 11 games. He also led the nation in rushing that year.
34. Woody Green who played with White's son, Danny
35. Paul Justin, 534 yards vs. Washington State in 1989
36. In Sept. of 1996, Jake Plummer passed Danny White's 6717 yards (1971-73).
37. Heading into the 1996 season, Danny White had 64 TD passes (1971-73), he was being closely pursued by Jake Plummer.
38. At press time, Jake Plummer was expected to surpass Danny White's 7257 yards (1971-73) in 1996.
39. Wilford "Whizzer" White, 347 yds. Against Idaho in 1950, White had 167 yds. rushing, 65 yds. passing, 75 yds. pass receiving, and 40 yds. kickoff returns. That season, the amazing "Whizzer" White compiled 2152 yds. He also holds the record for most touchdowns scored in a season, 22, and shares the most individual points scored in a season, 136. Incidentally, he also holds the record for the longest kickoff return. In 1948, against Pepperdine, White returned a kickoff 103 yds.
40. John Henry Johnson and Charley Taylor
41. Frank Kush (1994)

BASEBALL

1. Eddie Bane. On March 2, 1973, against Cal-Northridge. He also struck out 19. Of the seven Sun Devils who have thrown no-hitters, Bane is the only one to pitch in the major leagues.
2. Barry Bonds
3. Winkle's #1 and McDowell's #00 are the only jerseys that have been retired. (Reggie Jackson's major league number, 44, is also retired.)
4. The same jersey number, 24
5. Roger Schmuck, currently head baseball coach at Mesa Community College
6. Sterling Slaughter
7. Rick Monday (1965)
8. Bump Wills, Texas Ranger rookie in 1977 and son of former Dodger, Maury Wills
9. Bobby Winkles
10. Jim Brock
11. Bob Horner. (1986. Several major leaguers have hit four home runs in a game but Horner is the only one whose team lost the game.)
12. All were number one draft

picks. Monday '65, A's; Bannister '76, Astros; and Horner '78, Braves

13. They are the only Sun Devils to go directly from college to the major leagues. (Overall, only 17 drafted players have gone directly to the majors.)

14. All signed national letters-of-intent to attend ASU but opted to go professional instead.

15. Gary Gentry

16. Bob Horner (25). He also holds the ASU career record with 56 homers.

17. Floyd Bannister, Larry Gura and Kendall Carter all won 19 games.

18. All starters pitched the entire season without recording a loss.

19. Sterling Slaughter, the first Sun Devil to reach the major leagues (Cubs).

20. Kendall Carter and Craig Swan both won 47 games.

21. Reggie Jackson

22. Packard Stadium

23. Grand Canyon College (University)

24. Gary Gentry, 229 in 1965

WOMEN'S GOLF
1. JoAnn Gunderson Carner

MEN'S GOLF
1. Billy Mayfair
2. Phil Mickelson

WOMEN'S TENNIS
1. Anne Pittman

TRACK
1. Senon "Baldy" Castillo
2. Mile Relay Team

Wilford "Whizzer" White— was a star running back at Mesa High School and at ASU before going on to play for the Chicago Bears in the 1950's.

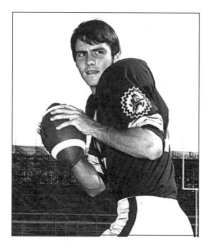

Top Left: **Danny White**

Top Right: **Reggie Jackson**

Left: **Rick Monday** (L) and coach **Bobby Winkles**

Bottom Left: **Bob Horner**

Bottom Right: **Jim Palmer**

Northern Arizona University Sports Trivia

1. Name the football coach who was the college coach of both Super Bowl XXX quarterbacks. (Troy Aikman, Dallas and Neil O'Donnell, Pittsburgh.)
2. Northern Arizona University is the only college in America to host both an NFL team and an NBA team for preseason training camps. Name these two teams.
3. How many universities in the country have their own domed stadiums, such as the J. Lawrence Walkup Skydome at Northern Arizona University?
4. Who is the all-time leading rusher in NAU football?
5. What are the official Northern Arizona University colors?
6. Which college athletic conference does NAU belong to?
7. As of June 1996 how many NAU football players had been drafted by the NFL?
8. Who is the All-American wide receiver from NAU who was drafted by Atlanta in 1988 and became a star in the NFL? He signed to play with the New Orleans Saints in 1994.
9. Who is the three-time All-American multi-purpose NAU

Jeff Lewis—former NAU quarterback.
(Photo courtesy NAU Sports Dept.)

football player (1979-83) who later starred in the NFL for the Detroit Lions, Green Bay Packers and Kansas City?

10. Who holds the NAU record for most all-purpose yardage in a career?

11. What was the original name of Northern Arizona University?

12. Who is generally considered as the greatest football coach in NAU history? (He coached for nine seasons, 1956-64.)

13. Who is the most prolific passer in NAU history?

14. Who is the NAU quarterback who was drafted in 1995 by the Denver Broncos?

15. NAU is also known as The _____ Campus.

16. What type of playing surface are football games played on inside the Skydome?

17. Who was the first player in NAU history to be drafted by the NFL in the first round?

18. Who was the coach of the NAU football team that went to the Holiday Bowl in Florida for the NAIA Championship in 1958?

Northern Arizona University
Sports Trivia Answers

1. Steve Axman, who became head coach at NAU.
2. Arizona Cardinals (NFL) and Phoenix Suns (NBA)
3. Eight, including NAU.
4. Allan Clark (1975-78), 2,723 yards. (At press time Archie Amerson was poised to become the new leader.)
5. Blue and Gold
6. Big Sky Conference
7. 32
8. Michael Haynes
9. Pete Mandley
10. Pete Mandley
11. Northern Arizona Normal School (1899)
12. Max Spilsbury. His teams went 59-24-5. The 1958 team was undefeated, losing in the NAIA national championship.
13. Greg Wyatt (1986-89)
14. Jeff Lewis
15. NAU is also called "The Mountain Campus."
16. Football games at the NAU Skydome are played on AstroTurf.
17. Shawn Collins
18. Max Spilsbury

Grand Canyon University Trivia

Grand Canyon University in Phoenix, has an enrollment that has only recently reached 1800 students. Despite its size the school has had a major impact on college baseball and basketball. Relying mostly on local talent, the school has sent more than 40 baseball players into the professional ranks including Tim Salmon, Chad Curtis, John Patterson, Kevin Wickander, Paul Swingle, and Brett Merriman. Between the years 1980-1986 the Antelopes won four N.A.I.A national championships.

1. Grand Canyon won the 1988 N.A.I.A. basketball championship. Who was their coach?
2. Name the former Phoenix Sun who holds Grand Canyon's career record for all of the following: Points Scored, 2195; Most Field Goals, 911; Most Free Throws Made, 373; Most Rebounds, 1544; Most Games Played, 122; and Most Games Started, 122.
3. Name the former star basketball player and coach at Grand Canyon who was later head coach of the University of Arizona Wildcats.
4. What is the mascot for Grand Canyon University?
5. Who holds the career record for home runs for Grand Canyon baseball?
6. Name the 1993 American League Rookie of the Year? He is one of only four to be selected unanimously by the Baseball Writers, the others preceding him were Carlton Fisk, Mark McGwire, and Sandy Alomar, Jr.
7. Name the first California Angel to be selected Rookie of the Year.

Grand Canyon University Trivia Answers

1. Paul Westphal
2. Bayard Forrest (1972-1976)
3. Ben Lindsay
4. Antelopes
5. Tim Salmon, 51 (1987-1989)
6. Tim Salmon
7. Tim Salmon

Cactus League Trivia

1. Name the two original teams in the Cactus League.

2. Who was the colorful owner of the Cleveland Indians who is remembered as the "Father of the Cactus League"?

3. The first Cactus League game was played in Tucson on March 8, 1947, between the Indians and Giants. The Indians won 3-1. Which future Hall of Famer was the winning pitcher?

4. Name the year and first Arizona-trained team to win a World Series.

5. Name the American League's first African-American ballplayer.

6. In 1951 the New York Giants traded spring training bases for a year with which team?

7. Who was the Phoenix contractor who owned the Yankees in 1951.

8. Name the future Hall of Famer who broke in with the Giants in 1951.

9. The 1951 spring training camp in Phoenix was the last for which great Yankee Hall of Famer?

10. The 1951 spring training camp in Phoenix was the first for which great Yankee Hall of Famer?

11. Name the third team to train in Arizona. They came to Mesa in 1952.

12. The Arizona spring training circuit officially became the Cactus League in 1954 when _____.

13. When was the first time two Cactus League teams met in a World Series?

14. Name Charlie Briley's downtown Scottsdale restaurant that was dubbed the "Watering Hole for the Pros".

15. Training in Mesa, the Oakland A's were three-time world champions in 1972-73-74. Name three former Arizona State University players who starred on that dynasty.

16. Name the chewing gum magnate owner of the Chicago Cubs.

17. Name the Mesa rancher who played a leading role in

bringing spring training baseball to the Valley. Hint: A stadium is named in his honor.

18. What is the name of the spring training ballpark in Tucson; also featured in the movie *"Major League"*?

19. Who hit the first home run in the old Scottsdale Stadium?

20. Name the east Mesa "spa" that was, for 25 years, the Giants headquarters as a prelude to spring training.

21. The 1954 Indians won a record 111 games (154-game season). Name their "Four Aces" pitching staff.

22. What was the name of the first franchise in Seattle?

23. That team left Seattle in 1971 and became the_____?

24. In 1977, Seattle got a new franchise and became the_____?

25. What is the name of the Cleveland Indians popular mascot?

26. 1960 Spring Training in Scottsdale was the last season for this Boston Red Sox "Splendid Splinter."

27. Name the first Cactus League team to win a World Series.

28. Name the Casa Grande baseball complex, built in 1961, that was used for many years by the San Francisco Giants.

29. Name the 1962 expansion team that trained in Apache Junction.

30. Name the future Hall of Famer who, in 1961, replaced Ted Williams in the Red Sox outfield.

31. Name the first team to train in Scottsdale.

32. Name the future Hall of Famer who broke into the starting lineup with the Orioles at spring training in Scottsdale in 1958.

33. Name the Phoenix civic group that was formed in 1937 to bring major league spring training to Arizona.

34. Name the historic Phoenix hotel that, during the early years was headquarters for the Giants (and Yankees in 1951).

35. Name the historic Tucson hotel that was headquarters for the Indians during the early years.

36. What is the name of the stadium in Chandler?

37. Which major league team now trains in Tucson?

38. Name the stadium in Tempe.

39. Which Cactus League team was owned by a legendary singing cowboy movie star? (Note: The team was sold to Disney in 1996.)

40. Who hit the first home run in the new Scottsdale Stadium?

41. Name the player who spent his entire 22-year career with Chicago and was known as "Mr. Cub."

42. Hall of Famer Henry Aaron played his last season with which Cactus League team?

43. He's "Baseball's Oldest Man In Uniform." At 92 he was Babe Ruth's roommate on the Yankees in the 1920s and seven decades later he was still hitting fungoes to the California Angels. Who is he?

44. Reggie Jackson played for three teams that are either in or were in the Cactus League. Name them.

Ryne Sandberg — All-Star 2nd baseman, Chicago Cubs (1982-present)

(Photo courtesy National Baseball Library, Cooperstown, NY.)

Cactus League Trivia Answers

1. New York (San Francisco) Giants and the Cleveland Indians (1947)
2. Bill Veeck
3. Bob Lemon
4. Cleveland Indians, 1948
5. Larry Doby, Cleveland Indians, July, 1947
6. New York Yankees
7. Del Webb
8. Willie Mays
9. Joe DiMaggio
10. Mickey Mantle
11. Chicago Cubs
12. A fourth team, the Baltimore Orioles began training in Yuma
13. 1954. Indians and the Giants. Giants won 4-0.
14. Pink Pony
15. Sal Bando, Rick Monday and Reggie Jackson
16. Philip K. Wrigley
17. Dwight Patterson
18. Hi Corbett Field
19. Ted Kluszewski of the Cincinnati Reds. (November 18, 1955)
20. Buckhorn Mineral Wells
21. Mike Garcia, Early Wynn, Bob Lemon and Bob Feller
22. Seattle Pilots
23. Milwaukee Brewers
24. Seattle Mariners
25. Wahoo (Cleveland Indians mascot)
26. Ted Williams
27. The 1954 New York Giants 4 games to 2 over Cactus League rival Cleveland. (Cleveland won the 1948 World Series. That was before the Cactus League.)
28. Francisco Grande
29. Houston Colt .45's
30. Carl Yastrezemski
31. Baltimore Orioles (1956)
32. Brooks Robinson
33. Thunderbirds
34. Adams Hotel
35. Santa Rita Hotel
36. Compadre Stadium
37. Colorado Rockies
38. Diablo Stadium
39. California Angels. (Gene Autry, who sold the team to Disney in 1996.)
40. Cory Snyder of the Giants (1992)
41. Ernie Banks
42. Milwaukee Brewers
43. Jimmie Reese
44. Baltimore, Oakland and California (The 1951 New York Yankees technically don't count because there was no official Cactus League at the time.)

Phoenix Suns Trivia

1. Name the 1993, Most Valuable Player in the NBA.
2. Which future NBA All Star did the 1969 Suns lose with the famous coin flip?
3. To which team did the Suns lose the coin flip in 1969?
4. What was the "most famous shot" ever made by a Suns player?
5. Who is associated with jersey #34 for the Phoenix Suns?
6. Who were the "Sun's twins"?
7. Who is the long-time "Voice of the Suns?"
8. Who replaced Johnny "Red" Kerr as coach in the 1969-70 season and again replaced Bill "Butch" van Breda Kolff in the 1972-73 season?
9. Which Suns player was known as the "Hawk" and wore jersey #42?
10. Michael Finley is his college's all time leading scorer with 2,147 points. Name that school.
11. Who was the first Sun selected to the NBA Hall of Fame?
12. Name the only trainer in Suns history.
13. Who was the "Original Sun", and later a Sun's color commentator?
14. What extremely rare event in a NBA basketball game at Veteran's Memorial Coliseum occurred on Oct. 6, 1974?
15. Name the Suns player killed in a plane crash in 1987.
16. Who is the Suns' longest tenured coach?
17. Who wore jersey #33?
18. What is "Cotton" Fitzsimmons' real first name?
19. Who wore jersey #44 for the Suns?
20. Who wore jersey #5 for the Suns?
21. Which two-time All Star for the Suns was traded for Boston's Rick Robey in what's considered the Suns' all-time worst trade?
22. How many games did the Suns win in their franchise-best

season in 1993?

23. Name the popular All Star guard the Suns gave up in the trade for Charles Barkley.

24. In 1990, the Suns and Jazz played in the first regular season game outside North America. Where was the game held?

25. In round numbers, how many fans can be seated in the America West Arena?

26. Who popularized the phrase, "Madhouse on McDowell"?

27. What do Paul Westphal, Alvan Adams, Connie Hawkins, Walter Davis and Dick Van Arsdale have in common?

28. Name the two Suns who have won the NBA Rookie of the Year Award.

29. Who is the all-time leading scorer for the Suns?

30. Which Sun has the most NBA All-Star appearances?

31. Who wore Jersey #6 for the Suns?

32. What did Henry Mancini, Ed Ames, Andy Williams and Bobbie Gentry have in common?

33. Of the above, only one is still involved with the Suns. Name that person.

34. Who are the only players in the NBA to win a Most Valuable Player award and not play on a World Champion team?

35. Name the Phoenix Suns first coach.

36. In what year did the Phoenix Suns play their first game?

37. What accomplished jazz pianist is better known for his play-by-play broadcasting?

38. Name the Phoenix Suns coach who has coached the team during three different periods.

39. What is the mascot of the Phoenix Suns?

40. What coach led the Phoenix Suns to the 1976 NBA Championship finals?

41. Which popular guard is known as "KJ"?

42. What is "Thunder Dan's" last name?

43. Who are the tallest and shortest Suns players to date?

44. What four players did Houston trade for Charles Barkley in the 1996?

Phoenix Suns Trivia Answers

1. Charles Barkley
2. Lew Alcindor (Kareem Abdul-Jabbar)
3. Milwaukee Bucks
4. Garfield Heard, 1976 Game 5 finals in Boston triple overtime loss to Celtics
5. Charles Barkley
6. Dick and Tom Van Arsdale
7. Al McCoy
8. Jerry Colangelo
9. Connie Hawkins
10. Wisconsin
11. Connie Hawkins (1992)
12. Joe "Magic Fingers" Proski
13. Dick Van Arsdale
14. Rain and leaky roof canceled a game between Phoenix and Portland
15. Nick Vanos
16. John MacLeod (nearly 14 years)
17. Alvan Adams
18. Lowell
19. Paul Westphal
20. Dick Van Arsdale
21. Dennis Johnson aka "DJ"
22. 62 (regular season)
23. Jeff Hornacek (also Tim Perry and Andrew Lang)
24. Tokyo, Japan
25. 19,000
26. Al McCoy
27. Their retired jerseys hang in the rafters at the America West Arena.
28. Alvan Adams and Walter Davis
29. Walter Davis (15,666 points)
30. Walter Davis (6)
31. Walter Davis
32. They were the original owners of the Suns.
33. Andy Williams
34. Charles Barkley & David Robinson (Spurs)
35. Johnny Kerr
36. 1968
37. Al McCoy
38. Cotton Fitzsimmons
39. The Gorilla
40. John MacLeod
41. Kevin Johnson
42. Majerle
43. Nick Vanos (7'2", 260 lbs., 1985-1987) and Greg Grant (5'7", 145 lbs., 1989-1990).
44. Chucky Brown, Mark Bryant, Robert Horry and Sam Cassell

Michael Finley
(Photo courtesy Phoenix Suns)

Arizona Cardinals Trivia

1. Name the NFL Hall of Famer who was the longtime general manager of the Phoenix/Arizona Cardinals.
2. Who was the first coach of the Phoenix/Arizona Cardinals?
3. Who was the first quarterback for the Phoenix/Arizona Cardinals?
4. Who was the first player drafted by the Phoenix/Arizona Cardinals?
5. What is the oldest continuous franchise in the NFL?
6. What was the original name of the Cardinals?
7. How did the Cardinals acquire their name?
8. What is significant about the 1925 season?
9. In the historic 40-6 victory over the Chicago Bears on Thanksgiving Day 1929, name the player-coach who scored all 40 points on 6 TD's and 4 extra points.
10. During World War II, as a manpower and wartime emergency measure, the Cardinals combined with which other NFL team?
11. What was the team called?
12. Where did the Chicago Cardinals play their home games?
13. Who did the Cardinals defeat 28-21 in the 1947 NFL Championship game?
14. In 1960, the Cardinals left Chicago and moved where?
15. In 1974, the Cardinals made it to the NFC Finals, losing 30-14 to which team?
16. The St. Louis Cardinals became the Phoenix Cardinals in what year?
17. What do former Cardinal players Larry Wilson, Stan Mauldin, J.V. Cain and Marshall Goldsberg have in common?
18. What do Dick "Night Train" Lane, Larry Wilson, Jim Thorpe, Ollie Matson, Ernie Nevers and Charley Trippi have in common?
19. Before the Chicago Cardinals began operations in 1922,

they were known as the _____.

20. In March, 1994, the Phoenix Cardinals changed their name to _____.

21. Name the legendary Oklahoma Sooner coach who was a Cardinal coach in the 1970s.

22. Who is the top career scorer in Cardinal history?

23. Who was the Cardinals first round draft pick in 1965?

24. Who holds the Cardinals single game rushing record?

25. Who holds the Cardinals single game passing record?

26. Who holds the Cardinals single game receiving record?

Arizona Cardinals
Trivia Answers

1. Larry Wilson
2. Gene Stallings
3. Neil Lomax
4. Ken Harvey
5. Arizona Cardinals (Racine, Chicago, St. Louis and Phoenix)
6. Morgan Athletic Club (1898 in Chicago)
7. In 1901, the Cardinals acquired their name from used jerseys purchased from the University of Chicago. The color was faded maroon, prompting owner Chris O'Brian to declare, "That's not maroon, it's Cardinal red!"
8. The Cardinals won their first NFL title
9. Ernie Nevers
10. Pittsburgh Steelers
11. Card-Pitt
12. Comiskey Park
13. Philadelphia Eagles
14. St Louis
15. Minnesota Vikings
16. 1988
17. Their numbers have been retired by the club.
18. All are former Cardinal players in the Pro Football Hall of Fame.
19. Racine Cardinals
20. Arizona Cardinals
21. Bud Wilkinson
22. Jim Bakken, Kicker, 1,380 pts. (1962-1978) 282 FG, 534 PAT)
23. Joe Namath (He signed with the rival AFL Jets.)
24. John David Crow, (1960) 24 carries, 203 yards vs. Steelers.
25. Neil Lomax (1984) 468 yards, 37-46, vs Redskins
26. Sonny Randle (1962) 256 yds., 16 rec., 1 TD, vs. Giants

Hollywood, Entertainment and the Arts in Arizona

Back in those halcyon days before radio, movies and television, lectures were a popular form of entertainment in Arizona communities. They generally ranged from temperance to aesthetics to free love. Highbrows, or those pretending to be, listened attentively to the sonorous rhetoric of William Shakespeare, performed by actors like **Edwin Booth.** Gilbert and Sullivan operettas were performed by traveling acting troupes. One group toured Arizona in the early 1880's performing *Pirates of Penzance* and *H.M.S Pinafore.* In the cast was **Josephine Sarah Marcus.** In Tombstone she became Wyatt Earp's paramour and figured prominently in the events leading up to the "Gunfight at OK Corral."

One night in Tombstone, during the ever-popular *Uncle Tom's Cabin,* a drunken cowboy pulled his six-shooter and plugged one of Simon Legree's dogs as it was chasing little Eliza across the stage. The marshal saved the puncher from an angry crowd and hauled him off to jail. He returned the next day, sober, and offered the troupe his horse as recompense.

Another popular form of entertainment was boxing. Matches were usually held in saloons and the rounds lasted until somebody went down. A thirty-second rest was called before beginning the next round. Fights could last more than a hundred rounds.

It's hard to imagine but at the same time the Earps and Doc Holliday were stalking the Clanton's and McLaury's at the OK Corral, baseball teams from Bisbee, Tombstone and Fort Huachuca were engaged in spirited competition.

Rodeos were the most popular spectator sport in the cowtowns and drilling contests attracted the largest crowds in the mining towns. Both Prescott and Payson lay claim to staging the West's oldest rodeo. In the drilling contests, single-jack drillers competed to see who could drill the deepest hole in a block of granite in fifteen minutes. Double-jack drillers consisted of a team of drillers. One held the drill bit while the other swung the hammer. Contestants were revered much the same as sports heroes of today.

Fires were a constant threat to frontier communities whose structures were made of wood and energy came from kerosene and wood stoves. Each town had at least one volunteer fire company. Each company prided itself on being the fastest at pulling those hose carts. Races between hose companies were staged on holidays. Like most contests, betting on the outcome was nearly as important as competitive pride.

Animal fights, such as dog or cock fights, were popular with the gaming crowd. Badger fights were common as were battles between longhorn cattle and bears. In fact, there was almost every conceivable kind of animal fight.

Communities formed their own marching bands who performed the music of John Philip Sousa and others on holidays such as the Fourth of July.

Saloons were a favorite place for song and dance acts of the low-brow caliber. This was the genesis of what later became vaudeville. During his younger days, comedian **Eddie Foy** performed his act at Tombstone's Bird Cage Theater.

Tear-jerking melodramas were popular with audiences. During one show a mean landlord was threatening to evict a young woman from her home because she couldn't pay the rent. The act was so convincing a tearful old prospector made his way up to the stage and tossed his poke sack full of gold dust up to the lady saying, "Here, lassie, take this and pay the old____."

Hurdy Gurdy dance halls were popular among single men. Girls charged 25 cents a dance and a percentage for the 50-cent drinks. They could supplement their income by making other arrangements on their own. Sometimes the music was provided by a wheezy hand organ and at fancy places, a 3-piece orchestra, usually consisting of a piano, violin and cornet.

When one thinks of movies made in Arizona, images are conjured of cavalry troops riding among the towering spires and buttes of Monument Valley, a cowhand stopping to water his horse at Red Rock Crossing in Oak Creek, or a gunfight on the dusty streets of Old Tucson.

Westerns aren't the only movies shot in Arizona. Arizona's wide open spaces have also been the setting for a wide variety of films featuring UFO encounters, car chases, inter-galactic adventures, comedies, and love stories.

During the 1992-93 fiscal year 18 feature-length movies were filmed, 66 major television projects, 340 national and international commercials, and 75 documentary and industrial projects were completed.

Flagstaff almost became the movie capital of the world. Back in 1911, **Jesse Lasky** and **Cecil B. De Mille** packed up their New York film production company and headed west to start a new film colony. The site they chose was Flagstaff, Arizona. But, when they arrived they were greeted by the chilly winds that typically blew snow, sleet and rain down off the lofty San Francisco Peaks. The two future movie moguls paused to re-consider, then packed their gear, got back on the train and headed further west, not stopping until they reached the Pacific Ocean.

The first motion picture with a story was Edwin S. Porter's *"The Great Train Robbery,"* filmed in the wilds of New Jersey in 1903. Audiences loved it and demanded more. Thus began America's long love affair with westerns.

Before the 1930's, very few people were aware of the wondrous beauty of Monument Valley but **Harry Goulding** would change all that. Goulding and his wife, **Mike,** operated a trading post in the valley. The Navajo were experiencing hard times during the Great Depression and Harry knew filmmakers were looking for new, spectacular sites for their westerns. So, in 1938, he gathered some Josef Muench photographs and took them to Hollywood where he was able to convince director **John Ford** to use Monument Valley as the setting for his epic movie, *"Stagecoach."* At last the world was aware of Monument Valley, and Arizona. Ford returned to the valley in 1946 to film *"My Darling Clementine,"* where it served as the setting for Tombstone and the Earp-

Ben Johnson with Joann Dru—in *"Wagonmaster"*. Monument Valley, 1950.

(Photo courtesy Southwest Studies)

Clanton feud. During the late 1940's and early 1950's he filmed the famed cavalry triad, *"Fort Apache," "Rio Grande"* and *"She Wore A Yellow Ribbon."* Arizona resident, **Ben Johnson,** became one of Ford's stable of cowboy stars during this time. Johnson was also a World Champion rodeo cowboy. He won an Academy Award in *"The Last Picture Show,"* the only person in history to win both honors.

John Ford's contribution to the economic welfare of the Navajo is immeasurable. His films brought millions in tourist dollars and wages to the Navajo. In 1955, he was in the valley again to film *"The Searchers,"* arguably the best western ever made.

Today, Monument Valley is the embodiment of what most people perceive when they visualize the Old West.

In 1939, "Old Tucson" was built next to the spectacular Saguaro National Monument for the film, *"Arizona."* It was later the setting for dozens of films and television shows including *"Gunsmoke,"* and *"High Chaparral."* It was also one of the state's most popular tourist attractions until a disastrous fire swept through it in 1995 (it is being rebuilt).

In 1948, **Howard Hawks** directed the western classic, *"Red River,"* starring **John Wayne,** in southern Arizona. Texans were very indignant and upset with Hollywood for using the San Pedro River and the Arizona landscape to shoot a story about the Lone Star State. A few years later Hollywood did it again, this time using the country around Patagonia to film the Rodgers and Hammerstein Broadway musical classic, *"Oklahoma."*

Sedona was another of Hollywood's favorite movie settings. The spectacular, wind-sculpted, red rock country with a sparkling, crystal clear creek meandering through it was a wonderful setting for such movies as *"Broken Arrow,"* *"Johnny Guitar,"* and *"The Rounders."*

Several native Arizonans including **Rex Allen, Marty Robbins, Leo Carrillo, Linda Ronstadt, Travis Edmonson, Ted DeGrazia** and **Andy Devine** all hit the national spotlight as performers and artists. Allen, a native of Willcox, was the only Hollywood singing cowboy who could actually claim to be a real cowboy.

Rex Allen, Sr.—native of Willcox and the last of the singing cowboys with his horse Koko.

(Photo courtesy Southwest Studies)

Grammy Award-winning Robbins, a native of Glendale, was a country music legend. Carrillo, from Tucson and Devine, born in Flagstaff and raised in Kingman, had long careers in the movies. Ronstadt is a top recording artist in the pop, country and rock fields and Edmonson was half of the popular folk duo of the 1960's, "Bud and Travis." Legendary Southwestern artist, Ted DeGrazia, was born in Morenci.

Academy Award-winning director **Steven Spielberg**; "Mr. Las Vegas" **Wayne Newton**; rocker **Vincent Damon Furnier** aka **"Alice Cooper"**; rock singer **Stevie Nicks**; the original host of the *Tonite Show*, **Steve Allen**; actors **Jack Elam** and **Nick Nolte**; actresses

Valerie Perrine and **Lynda Carter** all grew up in the Phoenix area.

Many other nationally-known artists and performers now call Arizona home. These include **Hugh Downs, Glen Campbell, Bil Keane, Paul Harvey, Jane Russell, Joe Garagiola, Joe Beeler** and **Bob McCall.**

Back in the days before television, technicolor and epic westerns, Hollywood filmmakers came to Arizona to shoot westerns of the silent film era and the early two-reel "talkies." During the 1920's and 30's, shooting stars like **Tex Ritter** and **Tom Mix** were turning out "Oaters" around Prescott. Ritter also found romance in Prescott. He fell in love with and married a local girl, **Dorothy Fay Southworth.** Their son **John** also became a well-known movie and television actor.

The greatest cowboy shooting star of the 1920's was Tom Mix, America's first larger-than-life movie hero. Stories were circulated by his fertile-minded agent that Mix had been a Texas Ranger, fought in the Boer War in Africa, rode with the Rough Riders in the Spanish-American War in Cuba, fought alongside Pancho Villa in the Mexican Revolution and experienced a number of other hair-raising adventures. It was great copy and the fans loved it. Actually, Mix had done none of the above but he could ride a horse with the best of them. He was also a world-class showman. Moviegoers eagerly filled the theaters to see his films. During the 1920's Mix was making $17,000 a week, an unbelievable sum of money for the time.

Tom Mix had been a performer with Zach Miller's famous 101 Wild West Show where he'd become an expert horseman. According to Prescott native, **Budge Ruffner,** Mix liked to entertain the locals around Prescott by dropping his hat on the ground then, while riding his horse Tony at full speed, lean gracefully out of the saddle and pick it up. Mix made it look easy, so easy many of the youngsters in town saddled up their ponies and tried to imitate him. Quite a few fell off in the process and broke their arms. It was said the angry young mothers posed a bigger threat to Tom than any band of outlaws he'd ever had to face down.

Tom Mix Memorial—Near Florence.
(Photo courtesy Jeff Kida)

Arizona
"Hollywood" Trivia

1. Where was John Ford's 1939 classic film, *"Stagecoach,"* filmed?

2. The stage driver in *"Stagecoach"* was played by this Arizona native.

3. Although the setting for John Ford's 1946 film, *"My Darling Clementine,"* was Tombstone, where was the movie actually filmed?

4. Which town was the setting for the 1964, Henry Fonda-Glenn Ford film, *"The Rounders"*?

5. Of which Arizona legend was the 1949 film *"Lust For Gold"* concerned?

6. Which role did young Glenn Ford play in *"Lust For Gold"*?

7. Michael J. Fox went to this Arizona site to film *"Back to the Future: Part III,"* in 1989.

8. Which classic old Arizona hotel was the San Antonio theater setting for the 1971 Paul Newman film, *"The Life and Times of Judge Roy Bean"*?

9. Sterling Hayden and Joan Crawford filmed this 1954 western in Sedona.

10. William Holden and Jean Arthur starred in the first movie filmed at Old Tucson. What was it?

11. Shirley Jones and Gordon MacRae starred in this movie version of a Broadway classic in 1954, filmed near Patagonia.

12. Which famous stuntman was killed in 1986 at the Vermillion Cliffs while filming, *"Million Dollar Industry"*?

13. Name the movie actress who was actually kidnapped by a Native American who wanted to ride off into the sunset (and marry her) while she was in Flagstaff making a movie called appropriately enough, *"Wilderness Trail",* with Tom Mix.

14. Sally Kellerman filmed *"Rafferty and the Gold Dust*

Twins" at this famous old saloon-restaurant in Cave Creek.

15. Which venerable Arizona landmark was "blown up" in *"McKenna's Gold"?*

16. Name the only film Marilyn Monroe made in Arizona.

17. What was the last picture John Wayne filmed in Arizona?

18. Name the only film Elvis Presley made in Arizona.

19. *"The Last Outpost,"* filmed in 1950, starred which actor?

20. The 1988 film *"Major League"* featured which Arizona ballpark?

21. The 1950 movie filmed in Sedona-Oak Creek, *"Broken Arrow"*, starring Jeff Chandler and James Stewart was about which two real-life Arizona figures?

22. Barbra Streisand's only film made in Arizona was?

23. *"Broken Lance"* was this legendary actor's only film made in Arizona.

24. In 1926, *"Son of the Sheik"* filmed in Arizona and starred?

25. In the 1991 Jean Claude Van Damme movie, *"Universal Soldier,"* which small Arizona town was virtually destroyed?

26. Name the famous Hollywood character-actor born in Flagstaff and raised in Kingman.

27. Name this Pulitzer-Prize winning political cartoonist for *The Arizona Republic* newspaper.

28. Fortieth Street and Camelback in Phoenix was the location for this western movie set during the 1950's.

29. What was the title of the series about the Arizona Rangers that was filmed there?

30. Who played the bad little kid, Gerald, on the *Wallace and Ladmo Show?*

31. Name this popular movie tough guy and star of such films as: *"The Deep," "48 Hours," "Prince of Tides,"* and *"Blue Chips"* who attended Phoenix College in the early 1960's.

32. Name the Tucson high school student, leader of the legendary "Sons of the Pioneers" who wrote the western music classic, *Tumbling Tumbleweeds.*

33. Name the Arizona resident who was an original member

of the New Christy Minstrels and is today the state's Official Balladeer.

34. In 1912, the same year Arizona became a state, name the classic cowboy song written in New York about an Arizona cowboy character.

35. This early-day Phoenix television personality hosted a variety show and helped launch the careers of Wayne Newton, Duane Eddy, Linda Day George, Lynda Carter, Linda Ronstadt, Tanya Tucker and others.

36. Name the Scottsdale Arcadia High student who played "Wonder Woman" on TV.

37. Name the entertainer who recorded *"By The Time I Get To Phoenix"* who now makes his home there.

38. Along which Arizona river was the classic western, *"Red River"* starring John Wayne and Montgomery Clift filmed?

39. In 1983, Harrison Ford starred in what blockbuster movie, part of which was filmed in Arizona?

40. Name the pop-rock singer from a pioneer Tucson family.

41. Name the popular bad-guy, character actor from Globe who graduated from Phoenix Union High and was famous as the "Face That Sunk A Thousand Stagecoaches." He appeared in dozens of westerns including, *"Once Upon A Time In The West," "The Apple Dumpling Gang"* and *"Rio Lobo."*

42. Name the former Arizona cowboy who starred in many films including, *"The Grey Fox," "Comes A Horseman" "Misery," "The Getaway,"* and *"Tom Horn."*

43. This son of migrant farm workers was inducted into the Country Music Hall of Fame in 1993. He co-starred on TV's Hee Haw, and his first hit was *"Under Your Spell Again."*

44. Who were the 1950's Phoenix TV entertainers known as the "Rascals in Rhythm"?

45. Best-known for his "twangy guitar," this Arizonan sold more than 100 million records and was inducted into Rock and Roll Hall of Fame, 1994.

46. This Phoenix attorney acted as child host on Lew King's *First Federal Ranger* television show in the 1950's.

47. Name the native Arizonan, author, cowboy singer, story-teller and trivia-maker who began his career in the 1960's with the folk-singing trio, Gin Mill Three.

48. John Ford along with his cast and crew headquartered at this trading post while filming his many westerns at Monument Valley.

49. Name the Hollywood cowboy killed in car crash in 1940 near Florence.

50. Which town was the setting for the 1985 Sally Field-James Garner film, *"Murphy's Romance?"*

51. Which Arizona hotel served as the plush Chicago hotel in the Glenn Ford-Jack Lemmon film, *"Cowboy?"*

52. In which Arizona town did Jesse Lasky and Cecil B. DeMille plan to establish a movie colony in 1911? (Hint: The cold weather chased them on to sunny southern California.)

53. Name the well-known character actor who has a street in Kingman named after him.

54. Arizona's "Singing Cowboy" Rex Allen calls this place his hometown.

55. Dorothy Fay Southworth, from a distinguished Prescott family, married this singing cowboy.

56. Which of the George Lucas films in the Star Wars group was shot near Yuma?

57. In 1994, Mel Gibson, Jodie Foster and James Garner filmed a movie version of which old television series in the vicinity of Lake Powell and Monument Valley?

58. This 1957 graduate of North Phoenix High School, by way of Holbrook, had a million-seller teeny bopper record called *"Plaything."* He appeared twice on Dick Clark's "American Bandstand." His rugged, all-American good looks and blond crew cut made him a natural teen idol. He later attended ASU on a football scholarship. Today, he teaches school in Tempe and entertains at Valley night-clubs.

59. Name this territorial Arizona native whose cartoons appeared in *Arizona Highways Magazine* in the 1930's. He was born in Duncan where he worked for nearly 50

years as an artist and cartoonist. He still paints today in Tubac.

60. This Phoenix guitarist and studio musician was known around the world of rock-a-billy and country music as the "Godfather of Phoenix-area guitarists." He played with many of the great entertainers of the time including Elvis Presley and was *mentor primero* to Rock and Roll Hall of Famer, Duane Eddy.

61. Name the best-selling Arizona author whose protagonist is a swashbuckling hero named Dirk Pitt.

62. Name the Phoenix radio personality who was host on the Tonight Show when it debuted on September 27, 1954.

63. Name this Phoenix native who recorded the 1965 hit song, *"Queen of the House"* along with other hits including, *"He's So Fine,"* and *"Baby I'm Yours."*

64. What Arizona town does famous clown, Emmett Kelley Jr. call his hometown?

65. What did author Zane Grey call his novel set in Oak Creek Canyon?

66. Kino Springs, near Nogales, was the home for these English-born husband-wife movie stars.

67. Name this native of Morenci who became internationally known for his unique depictions of the Southwest. His paintings are seen on everything from lithographs and prints to collector plates and refrigerator magnets.

68. What city played host to movie companies during the filming of *Flight of the Phoenix; Road to Morocco; Road to Zanzibar; Beau Geste; Return of the Jedi;* and *Raiders of the Lost Ark?*

69. Name two epic movies about the "Sooner State" that were actually filmed in Arizona.

70. Which Arizona lake was the Sea of Gallilee in *"The Greatest Story Ever Told"* (1965)?

71. In 1975, Travis Walton of Snowflake was allegedly abducted by a UFO. Hollywood made a movie of his experiences in 1993. Name the movie.

72. Which movie made in Arizona in 1955 about another state caused a movement by some citizens in that state to

boycott the movie?

73. Name the author of the books, *Flight of the Phoenix* and *The Quiller Memorandum,* who was a resident of Arizona.

74. In the movie *The Mountain* (1956) starring Robert Wagner and Spencer Tracy, which Arizona mountains represented, in close-ups, the Swiss Alps?

75. The movie *McClintock* (1962), starring John Wayne and Maureen O'Hara, was filmed at which famous old Spanish Land Grant ranch?

76. Hollywood actress, Oscar-winner, Anne Baxter, was the granddaughter of what famous architect?

77. Name this science-fiction writer who calls Tucson his home town. He was the author of the classic novel *Fahrenheit 451* and scripted the first episode of *Twilight Zone.* His short story, *The Veldt,* foreshadowed virtual reality. He has produced more than 500 works—novels, short stories, screenplays, teleplays and poetry.

78. Name this prodigy of Kingman. He was a satirical cartoonist for the *New Times,* a Valley radio personality and author of books on Billy the Kid, Wyatt Earp, Doc Holliday and Geronimo.

79. Who was ASU's Pulitzer-Prize winning poet?

80. Name the author of *The Trunk Murderess: Winnie Ruth Judd.*

81. Name the author of *A Marriage Made in Heaven, or, Too Tired for an Affair.* She was also one of America's most popular newspaper columnists.

82. Name this nationally syndicated cartoonist who draws *Family Circus.* His cartoons are read daily by an estimated 100 million people and he has 14 million books in print.

83. Name this husband-wife team who photograph and write on cultures of the Southwest. Their work appears in *Arizona Highways Magazine* and they are the authors of *Beyond Tradition: Contemporary Indian Art and Its Evolution.*

84. Name this host of ABC News' *20/20.* He also hosted the

Tonight Show and the *Today Show.* His awards include two Emmy Awards for investigative reporting. He holds the record for the greatest number of hours on network commercial television.

85. A popular folk duo of the 60's, *"Bud and Travis"*, featured this Nogales native.

86. Name this former columnist for *The Arizona Republic,* editor for *Arizona Highways Magazine* and author of several books including, *A Mile in His Moccasins* and *A Little War of Our Own.*

87. Country music legend Marty Robbins' wife, also a native Arizonan, had a most unusual name. What was it?

88. In what famous Arizona hotel was Janet Leigh staying for the opening of scenes, and just prior to, the classic shower scene in the movie *"Psycho"*?

89. Who was the Wyoming-bred daughter of an Arapaho mother and French/English father. She modeled in New York then went to Hollywood and appeared mostly in jungle movies and Westerns. She later appeared on local television, advertising cars.

90. He came here in the 1940's for his health. While in college (Arizona State) he was hired to work at radio station KOY as a disc jockey, newsman and soap opera actor. He was later a Hollywood actor, comedian, musician and television host. Who was he?

91. This long-time resident of Tubac was the son of a famous American humorist, movie actor, stage performer and writer. He played the role of his father in the Hollywood biography of his late father.

92. Which folk icon spent a "secret year" (1972), in the Salt River Valley? He once held an impromptu folk concert while tubing down the Salt.

93. This Cortez High School graduate's real name is Vincent Damon Furnier and he is considered the "granddaddy of punk rock."

94. What is the name of Rex Allen's horse?

95. She appeared as "Miss Kitty" in the long-running television series, *"Gunsmoke."* She lived in the Salt River

Valley from 1964 to 1984.

96. This veteran radio news personality could give you the "rest of the story" from his Carefree home.

97. This former major league baseball player was a catcher for the World Champion St. Louis Cardinals in 1946. He was also a baseball broadcaster and television host.

98. Name one of the three "Cavalry Triad" John Wayne films made in Monument Valley.

99. What character did Warner Baxter play to win his 1929 Academy Award in the film *In Old Arizona?*

100. What was Arizona's first licensed commercial radio station?

101. What was the occasion of the first motion picture recording of a Presidential event?

102. Name the Phoenix author of the popular book *The Curse of the Dutchman's Gold.*

103. Name the hometown of country music legend Marty Robbins.

104. What is the state song of Arizona?

105. What illustrious artists' group was founded in Oak Creek Tavern in Sedona by Joe Beeler, John Hampton, George Phippen and Charlie Dye?

106. Who wrote, *The Grass is Always Greener Over the Septic Tank* and *If Life is a Bowl of Cherries What am I Doing in the Pits?*

107. What are Carlos Elmer, Ray Manley and David Muench best known for?

108. What 1950's Western epic starred Jeff Chandler and James Stewart?

109. Who wrote *Riders of the Purple Sage* and *Under the Tonto Rim?*

110. What is songwriter Bobby Troup best remembered for in Arizona?

111. Name the Italian miner's son who grew up in Morenci and became a famous artist.

112. What native Arizona folksinger is known for her songs about the Colorado River and working cowboys?

113. What were the Fox and the Orpheum?

114. Name the Scottsdale author who wrote, *The Shootist, Bless the Beasts and Children,* and *Where the Boys Are.*

115. Name this former opera singer and musician who became Arizona's first prime-time news anchorwoman.

116. Who is Arizona's official balladeer?

117. What famous movie star owned the 26 Bar Ranch in Arizona?

118. What was Navajo artist Carl Gorman during WWII?

119. What noted black and white photographer's photo collection is housed at the UofA's Center for Creative Photography? (His initials were A.A.)

120. What was the first movie filmed at Old Tucson in 1939?

121. What movie shot at Old Tucson starred John Wayne and Walter Brennan?

122. Name the long-running TV show founded by former Phoenix resident (North High School) Joan Ganz Cooney who also founded the Children's Television Workshop.

123. Which movie star was known as the "Arizona Cowboy?"

124. Name this popular Phoenix meteorologist, almanac author, and former state legislator.

125. Where was the movie *Junior Bonner,* starring Steve McQueen, filmed?

126. What name was Zane Grey born with?

127. Who was the author of *Desert Solitaire* and *The Monkey Wrench Gang?*

128. Name Arizona's biggest selling female recording artist.

129. What Arizona movie featured Kirk Douglas, Burt Lancaster, John Ireland and DeForrest Kelly?

130. What was the title of Marguerite Noble's best-selling novel on the Tonto Basin?

131. Name this cartoonist who graduated from Phoenix Union High School just prior to World War II. In Europe, writing for *Stars and Stripes,* he created the grungy combat characters "Willie and Joe." The series, *"Up Front"* was later made into a movie by the same name. He won two Pulitzer Prizes for his work.

132. What movie cowboy of the early 1900's was the first to carry two six-shooters?

133. What famous 1939 movie starred William Holden and Jean Arthur?

134. What highway's name in Arizona is glorified in a Gordon Lightfoot song?

135. What TV show, that ended in 1989, was the nation's longest running TV show with the original cast?

136. What scenes does Arizona artist Robert McCall paint?

137. Who hosted the TV series *Death Valley Days* near Apache Junction in the 1960's?

138. Name the founding member of the Cowboy Artists of America who painted *"Tyin' Knots in the Devil's Tail"*.

139. Who is always "On the Arizona Road?"

140. What was the name of John Wayne's first major Arizona film?

141. Which site has graced the front cover of *Arizona Highways Magazine* the most times?

142. Who played Arizona Ranger Captain Tom Rynning on the 1950's TV show, *26 Men?*

143. What was Arizona's first television station?

144. Who is "The Lion of Tombstone"?

145. Complete the following from Bobby Troup's classic song *"Get Your Kicks on Route 66"*: Flagstaff, Arizona and don't forget _____.

146. Who is Cara Jackson?

147. The 1983 movie classic, *"A Christmas Story,"* was a story about a little boy who yearned for a Red Ryder BB gun for Christmas. Name the Phoenix resident at the time who starred as "Ralphie."

148. *"Stagecoach,"* directed by John Ford and starring John Wayne was the first major motion picture filmed in Monument Valley. What was the first picture done in technicolor?

149. Name two popular television entertainers on KPHO Channel 5 (Phoenix), who entertained children (and adults) for 35 years.

150. In 1990's movies, *"Wyatt Earp"* and *"Tombstone,"* Dennis Quaid and Val Kilmer played what famous gunfighter?

151. Name the 1947 John Wayne movie, filmed in Sedona, where a Quaker woman's love (played by Gail Russell) reforms an outlaw named Quirt.

152. Name the Wickenburg dude ranch owner who penned the western classic cowboy song, *"Blood on the Saddle."*

153. What cowboy singer-actor is identified with that song?

154. Zane Grey's novel, *"To The Last Man,"* was based on what famous Arizona range war.

155. Name this award-winning Native American sculptor-artist whose bold colored canvas paintings of the American Indian have been shown throughout the world.

156. Name the comic strip character created by Tucson cartoonist Fred Rhoades.

157. Who was the Arizona singer featured in the rock group Fleetwood Mac?

158. Name the author of *"Tobacco Road"* and other books located in the South, who spent the latter part of his life in Arizona.

159. Name the mystery writer that uses Navajo Tribal Police as protagonists.

160. Name the famous Hollywood couple who married in Kingman on March 30, 1939 and reputedly honeymooned in Oatman.

161. Name this artist-writer who left New York in 1915 and landed in Globe where he went on to write and illustrate such books as "Cowboy" and "Apacheland."

162. Name the Prescott native who, in 1917, penned the cowboy classic poem, "Tyin' Knots in the Devil's Tail." (Sierry Petes)

163. In 1968, Stephen Fromholtz was inspired to write the western classic song, *"Man With the Big Hat,"* while sitting in this Cave Creek Saloon.

Arizona "Hollywood" Trivia Answers

1. Monument Valley
2. Andy Devine

Andy Devine—native of Flagstaff and raised in Kingman.

3. Monument Valley
4. Sedona
5. The Lost Dutchman Mine
6. Jacob Waltz
7. Monument Valley
8. Gadsden Hotel in Douglas
9. *"Johnny Guitar"*
10. *"Arizona"*
11. *"Oklahoma"*
12. Dar Robinson
13. Coleen Moore. (She was able to escape her would-be suitor after a wild ride in the wilderness.)
14. Harold's Cave Creek Corral
15. Spider Rock in Canyon de Chelly
16. *"Bus Stop"* (1956)
17. *"Rio Lobo"*
18. *"Stay Away Joe"* (1967)
19. Ronald Reagan
20. Hi Corbett Field in Tucson

21. Cochise and Tom Jeffords
22. *"A Star Is Born."*
23. Spencer Tracy
24. Rudolph Valentino
25. Ashfork
26. Andy Devine
27. Steve Benson
28. Cudia City
29. *"Twenty-Six Men"*
30. Radio personality, Pat McMahan
31. Nick Nolte
32. Bob Nolan
33. Dolan Ellis
34. *"Ragtime Cowboy Joe"*
35. Lew King
36. Lynda Carter
37. Glen Campbell
38. The San Pedro
39. *"Raiders of the Lost Ark"*
40. Linda Ronstadt

Linda Ronstadt—native of Tucson. Pop, rock and roll and country recording artist.

41. Jack Elam
42. Richard Farnsworth
43. Buck Owens
44. Wayne and Jerry Newton
45. Duane Eddy
46. Gary Peter Klahr
47. Marshall Trimble
48. Gouldings Trading Post on the Arizona-Utah border.
49. Tom Mix
50. Florence
51. The Gadsden Hotel in Douglas.
52. Flagstaff
53. Andy Devine
54. Willcox
55. Tex Ritter (They are the parents of actor John Ritter.)
56. *"Return of the Jedi"*
57. *"Maverick"*
58. Ted Newman
59. Hal Empie
60. Al Casey
61. Clive Cussler
62. Steve Allen
63. Jody Miller
64. Tombstone
65. *"Call of the Canyon."* The book was made into a movie in 1923 using Sedona and Oak Creek as the setting. It was the first of many movies made in the spectacular red rock country.
66. Stewart Granger and Jean Simmons
67. Ettore "Ted" De Grazia
68. Yuma
69. *"Oklahoma"* (1955) and *"Cimarron"* (1959)
70. Lake Powell
71. *"Fire in the Sky"*
72. *"Oklahoma"* It's worth mentioning that the films *"Cali-*

fornia" and *"Albuquerque"* were also filmed in Arizona.
73. Elleston Trevor
74. Superstition Mountains
75. San Rafael de la Zanja, later owned by the famous copper baron, Colonel William C. Greene.
76. Frank Lloyd Wright
77. Ray Bradbury
78. Bob Boze Bell
79. Rita Dove. She is now America's Poet Laureate at the Library of Congress.
80. Jana Bomersbach
81. Erma Bombeck
82. Bil Keane
83. Jerry and Lois Jacka
84. Carefree resident Hugh Downs.
85. Travis Edmonson

Travis Edmonson—native of Nogales. Member of the popular 1960's folk duo "Bud & Travis"

John Wayne—owned the 26 Bar Ranch in Eagar, Arizona

86. Don Dedera
87. Marizona Robbins. She was born in Maricopa County, Arizona, hence, "Marizona."
88. The old Jefferson Hotel in downtown Phoenix
89. Acquanetta
90. Steve Allen
91. Will Rogers Jr.
92. Bob Dylan
93. Alice Cooper
94. Koko
95. Amanda Blake
96. Paul Harvey
97. Joe Garagiola. His wife Audrey was the organist at Sportsman's Park in St. Louis when Joe played there along with other Cardinal greats like Stan Musial, Enos Slaughter and Red Schoendienst.
98. *"She Wore a Yellow Ribbon," "Rio Grande"* and *"Fort Apache."*
99. The Cisco Kid
100. KFAD, now KTAR
101. President William H. Taft signing the bill admitting Arizona to statehood
102. Helen Corbin
103. Glendale
104. *"Arizona March Song"*, or *"Arizona"* by Rex Allen, Jr. (alternate song)
105. Cowboy Artists of America
106. Erma Bombeck
107. Their pictures. They are photographers.
108. *"Broken Arrow"* (filmed at Sedona)
109. Zane Grey
110. He wrote: *"Get Your Kicks on Route 66"*.
111. Ted DeGrazia
112. Katie Lee
113. Movie theaters (Phoenix)
114. Glendon Swarthout
115. Mary Jo West
116. Dolan Ellis
117. John Wayne
118. A Navajo Code Talker
119. Ansel Adams
120. *"Arizona"*

121. *"Rio Bravo"*
122. Sesame Street
123. Rex Allen
124. Ed Phillips
125. Prescott
126. Pearl Gray (spelled Gray)
127. Edward Abbey
128. Linda Ronstadt
129. *"Gunfight at the O.K. Corral"*
130. *"Filaree"*
131. Bill Mauldin
132. The Cisco Kid
133. *"Arizona"*
134. Carefree Highway
135. *"Wallace and Ladmo Show"*
136. Space, science and futuristic scenes
137. Ronald Reagan
138. George Phippen
139. Bill Leverton
140. *"Stagecoach"* (1939)
141. The Grand Canyon
142. Tris Coffin
143. KPHO, Channel 5
144. Wyatt Earp
145. Winona
146. The first African-American Miss Arizona, (1995)
147. Peter Billingsley
148. *"She Wore A Yellow Ribbon"* also directed by John Ford and starring John Wayne.
149. Wallace and Ladmo
150. Doc Holliday
151. *"Angel and the Badman"*
152. Romaine Lowdermilk
153. Tex Ritter
154. The Pleasant Valley War or The Graham-Tewksbury Feud.
155. Fritz Scholder
156. Sad Sack
157. Stevie Nicks
158. Erskine Caldwell
159. Tony Hillerman
160. Clark Gable and Carole Lombard
161. Ross Santee
162. Gail Gardner
163. Harold's Cave Creek Corral

Dolan Ellis—*Official Arizona State Balladeer.*

Ted Newman—*Author of the million-seller hit "Plaything"*

Arizona Glossary
(With Pronunciations)

The rich Spanish heritage and Native American cultures have had a great influence on the language in Arizona. Words like **Gila** (Hee-la), **Saguaro** (Sa-war-o) and **Mogollon** (Muggy-own) will humble even the most arrogant. In many parts of Arizona, when you mispronounce our words, the price of the margaritas goes up accordingly.

Spanish is a beautiful language and should be spoken correctly. An important thing to remember with Spanish is two "LL's" mean the word should be pronounced "Y." For example: tortilla is pronounced "tor-tee-ya," and rillito is "ree-yee-toe." A single "L" keeps the "L" sound. An example would be "alamo."

It's been said that Pancho Villa shot many a gringo for calling him "Mr. Vila," instead of "Mr. Vee-yah."

Also, the "J" in Spanish is pronounced with an "H" sound. **Ajo** is not "Aw-jo" but "Aw-ho." A story is told about an eastern tourist who was doing his best to fit in when he happened to stop in Ajo. There he met a man named Julian Javier, who patiently explained to the visitor that his name was pronounced "Hulian Havier."

"Tell me, Hoo-lian," the man ventured, after careful deliberation, "does it get hot here in Hune and Huly?" The story should end there—but wait—there's more! A short time later the visitor was having lunch in downtown Ajo. "How do you pronounce the name of this place?" he asked. She gave him a puzzled look, then replied very slowly, "Mc—Donalds!"

Here is a glossary of words you might encounter in your *journada* around Arizona:

Acequia: (Ah-sec-qui-a) Spanish for "ditch."

Agua caliente: (ah-gua cal-yen-tay) Spanish for "hot water."

Agua frio: (ah-gua free-yo) Spanish for "cold water."

Alta: (awl-tah) Spanish for "upper."

Ancha: (on-cha) Spanish for "broad."

Arroyo: (ah-roy-oh) Spanish for "gulch" or "gully."

Arroz: (a-rose) Spanish for "rice"

Bahaana: (ba-hon-ah) Hopi for "white people."

Baja: (baa-ha) Spanish for "lower."

Bilagaana: (bil-a-gone-a) Navajo for "white people."

Bonita: (bon-ee-tah) Spanish for "pretty."

Bosque: (boss-kay) (bossk) Spanish for "forest grove."

Bronco: (bron-co) Spanish for "wild."

Caballo: (cah-buy-oh) Spanish for "horse."

Camino: (cah-meen-oh) Spanish for "road" or "highway."

Cienega: (see-en-eh-guh) Spanish for a "marshy area."

Calle: (cah-yea) Spanish for "street."

Chaparral: (sha-par-al) Spanish for "scrub brush."

Cholla: (choy-ah) Spanish for "skull." Also a cactus.

Cobre: (co-bray) Spanish for "copper."

Cuidad: (see-you-dad) Spanish for "city."

Flatlander: A term used (never endearing) by rural Arizona mountain folks for residents of the Phoenix-Tucson area who invade their cool climes each summer.

Frijoles: (free-hole-ees) Spanish for "beans."

Frijoles Negros: (free-hole-ees neh-gros) Spanish for "black beans."

Gringos: (green-gos) Spanish for "foreigners."

Güero: (Gwe-ro) Spanish for "blonde."

Hogan: (ho-gahn) A circular dwelling made of earth and logs. A traditional Navajo home.

Jacale: (ha-cal-ee) Spanish for hut or primative dwelling.

Kiva: (kee-vah) An underground ceremonial chamber used by Pueblo Indians such as the Hopi.

Laguna: (lah-goon-ah) Spanish for "pond."

Libro: (Lee-bro) Spanish for "book."

Llano: (yawn-oh) Spanish for "plain."

Mesa: (may-sah) Spanish for "table" or "flat-top mountain."

Mesteno or **mustang:** (mess-teen-yo) or (mus-tang) Spanish for "wild stray."

Monsoon: (mon-soon) Arizona's rainy season: July, August and September.

Montana: (mon-tana) Spanish for "mountain."

Muchachas: (mu-cha-chas) Spanish for "girls."

Muchachos: (mu-cha-chos) Spanish for "boys."

Nevada: (knee-vad-a) Spanish for "snow-covered."

Ocotillo: (oh-cah-tee-yo) Spanish for "coach whip." Also a desert plant.

Oro: (o-row) Spanish for "gold."

Palo Verde: (pah-low vehr-de) Spanish for "green stick."

Picacho: (pee-ca-cho) Spanish for "peak."

Piñata: (peen-ya-tah) A colorful paper-maché decoration filled with candy.

Plata: (pla-tah) Spanish for "silver."

Poco: (po-ko) Spanish for "small."

Pueblo: (puay-blow) Spanish for "village."

Rillito: (ree-ey-to) Spanish for "creek."

Rio: (ree-oh) Spanish for "river."

Rodeo: (ro-day-o) Spanish for "roundup."

Rojo: (ro-ho) Spanish for "red."

Quien Sabe? (quen-sah-vee) Spanish for "who knows."

Sierra: (see-air-ah) Spanish for "saw-tooth ridges."

Snowbird: An endearing (usually) term for tourists who spend the winter in Arizona.

Tsegi: (sig-ie) Navajo for "canyon."

Vaquero: (va-quer-oh) Spanish for "cowboy." Also charro and caballero.

Vieja: (vee-ay-ha) Spanish for "old."

Wickiup: (wick-ee-up) An Apache dome-shaped dwelling made of brush or bear grass.

Zonie: An endearing (sometimes) term used by Californians for Arizonans who go there in the summer.

● **Trivia:** (tri-vee-ah) Everything you needed to know about Arizona, but were afraid to ask!

Index

Index to Photos

Suggested Reading List

Arizona Office of Tourism
1989 *Arizona Travel Planner.* Phoenix, AZ

Chronic, Halka
1983 *Roadside Geology of Arizona.* Mountain Press. Missoula, MT

Cook, James
1989 *Arizona Pathways: Trails of History.* Arizona Highways. Phoenix, AZ

Comeaux, Malcolm L.
1981 *Arizona.* Westview Press. Boulder, CO

Desert Botanical Garden Staff
1988 *Desert Flowers.* Arizona Highways. Phoenix, AZ

Lowe, Charles
1977 *Arizona's Natural Environment.* University of Arizona Press. Tucson, AZ

Manning, Reg
1985 *The Cactus Book: What Kinda Cactus Izzat?* Reganson Cartoon Books. Phoenix, AZ

Olin, George
1975 *Mammals of the Southwest Deserts.* Southwest Parks and Monuments Association. Tucson, AZ
1975 *Mammals of the Southwest Mountains and Mesas.* Southwest Parks and Monuments Association. Tucson, AZ
1977 *House in the Sun: Flora and Fauna of Arizona.* Southwest Parks and Monuments Association. Tucson, AZ

Phillips, Edward
1996 *Arizona Almanac.* KTAR. Phoenix, AZ

Stocker, Joseph
1995 *Travel Arizona.* Arizona Highways. Phoenix, AZ

Trimble, Marshall
1982 *Arizona Adventure.* Golden West Publishers. Phoenix, AZ
1985 *In Old Arizona.* Golden West Publishers. Phoenix, AZ
1986 *A Roadside History of Arizona.* Mountain Press. Missoula, MT
1989 *Arizoniana.* Golden West Publishers. Phoenix, AZ
1989 *Arizona: A Cavalcade of History.* Treasure Chest Publications. Tucson, AZ

Trimble, Marshall, Sam Negri and James Cook
1995 *The Backroads: Travel Arizona.* Arizona Highways. Phoenix, AZ

Weir, Bill
1981 *Arizona Handbook.* Moon Publications. Chico, CA

Willoughby, Jim, and Sue Willoughby
1993 *Cactus Country.* Golden West Publishers. Phoenix, AZ

About the Authors

Marshall Trimble — was born in Tempe, Arizona. His family later moved to the railroad town of Ashfork where he grew up. He still considers this northern Arizona community his hometown.

Marshall began his stage career as a folksinger and today appears frequently on television as a storyteller of Arizona folk history. A versatile personality, he is as comfortable performing on stage with his guitar as he is addressing a group of serious historians.

Marshall has taught Arizona and Southwest history at Scottsdale Community College since 1972 and authored more than a dozen books on Arizona. He is project director for Maricopa Community College's unique Southwest Studies Program.

Doug Clark — formed a partnership and friendship with Marshall Trimble when Doug created the Arizona Trivia® game several years ago. Marshall had a file full of information about Arizona and Doug had the expertise to complete the project.

Doug and his wife Christina are long-time residents of Arizona. Doug graduated from the University of Arizona and earned his MBA at Arizona State University.

More Books by Marshall Trimble

ARIZONA ADVENTURE

Daring deeds and exploits of Wyatt Earp, Buckey O'Neill, the Rough Riders, Arizona Rangers, and the notorious Tom Horn, to name a few. Read about the Power Brothers shootout, Pleasant Valley wars, the Hopi revolt—action-packed true tales of early Arizona!   5 1/2 x 8 1/2—160 pages . . . $6.95

IN OLD ARIZONA

Southwestern tales more thrilling than fiction. History comes to life with humor, pathos and irony. Pioneer lives, bungled burglaries, shady deals, frontier lawmen, the Baron of Arizona and more!   5 1/2 x 8 1/2—160 pages . . . $6.95

ARIZONIANA

The *Legend of Red Ghost, The Fabulous Lost Adams Diggings, Uncle Jim's Last Gunfight, Con Men of Yesteryear* and *Frank Murphy's Railroad* are only a few of the stories in this fascinating book.   5 1/2 x 8 1/2 — 160 Pages . . .$8.95

More Books by Golden West Publishers

ARIZONA LEGENDS & LORE

Stories of Southwestern pioneers by a master storyteller: *Mysterious Lady in Blue, Captivity of Olive Oatman, Dutchman's Gold, Vulture Gold, Sharlot Hall, Louisa Wetherill and the Navajos,* and more! By Dorothy Daniels Anderson.

5 1/2 x 8 1/2—176 pages . . . $6.95

EXPLORE ARIZONA!

Where to find old coins, bottles, fossil beds, arrowheads, petroglyphs, waterfalls, ice caves, cliff dwellings. Detailed maps to 59 Arizona wonders! By Rick Harris.

5 1/2 x 8 1/2— 128 pages . . . $6.95

GHOST TOWNS
and Historical Haunts in Arizona

Visit cities of Arizona's golden past, browse through many photographs of adobe ruins, old mines, cemeteries, ghost towns, cabins and castles! Come, step into Arizona's past! By prize-winning journalist Thelma Heatwole.

5 1/2 x 8 1/2—144 pages . . . $6.95

QUEST for the DUTCHMAN'S GOLD

Facts, myths and legends of the fabled Superstition Mountains as told by Robert Sikorsky, a nationally syndicated columnist. Includes maps and numerous photos.

5 1/2 x 8 1/2—160 pages . . . $6.95

TALES OF ARIZONA TERRITORY

True stories of Arizona's pre-statehood history, stagecoaches and stage stations. Adventures and misadventures of pioneers, lawmen, and desperadoes. By Charles D. Lauer.

5 1/2 x 8 1/2—176 pages . . . $6.95

ORDER BLANK

GOLDEN WEST PUBLISHERS

☼ 4113 N. Longview Ave. • Phoenix, AZ 85014

602-265-4392 • **1-800-658-5830** • FAX 602-279-6901

Qty	Title	Price	Amount
	Arizona Adventure	6.95	
	Arizona Cook Book	5.95	
	Arizona Crosswords	4.95	
	Arizona Legends & Lore	6.95	
	Arizona Outdoor Guide	6.95	
	Arizona Trivia	8.95	
	Arizoniana	8.95	
	Cactus Country	6.95	
	Discover Arizona!	6.95	
	Explore Arizona!	6.95	
	Fishing Arizona	7.95	
	Ghost Towns in Arizona	6.95	
	Hiking Arizona	6.95	
	Horse Trails in Arizona	9.95	
	In Old Arizona	6.95	
	Motorcycle Arizona!	9.95	
	Old West Adventures in Arizona	5.95	
	Prehistoric Arizona	5.00	
	Quest for the Dutchman's Gold	6.95	
	Tales of Arizona Territory	6.95	
Shipping & Handling Add ➠	U.S. & Canada	$2.00	
	Other countries	$5.00	

☐ My Check or Money Order Enclosed $

☐ MasterCard ☐ VISA ($20 credit card minimum)

(Payable in U.S. funds)

Acct. No.   Exp. Date

Signature

Name   Telephone

Address

City/State/Zip

9/96   **Call for FREE catalog**   AZ Trivia

This order blank may be photo-copied.